3

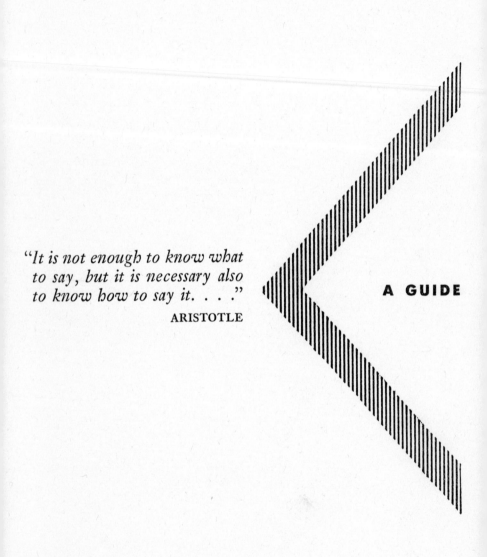

"It is not enough to know what to say, but it is necessary also to know how to say it. . . ."

ARISTOTLE

A GUIDE

SPEAKING
FOR RESULTS

FOR BUSINESS AND PROFESSIONAL SPEAKERS

RALPH A. MICKEN
Southern Illinois University

HOUGHTON MIFFLIN COMPANY · BOSTON
The Riverside Press Cambridge

INTRODUCTION

This book is intended to be practical. It assumes that the usefulness of speech is immediate. It works from the point of view that there is nothing to be ashamed of in speaking for results. It is aimed at the busy people in America who sell, promote, plan, and build. After all, in the whole social, industrial and political complex that is America nothing is more important than good talk. Speaking is not something that comes before doing; neither is it something that goes on instead of action. Rather it is a form of action. It *is* doing. In many situations the first thing to do is to talk matters over. When we marvel at an industry that produces millions of cars per year we know that many automobiles are made because that many can be sold. Hundreds of thousands of the people who put money into annuity policies would never have done so of themselves — they had to be sold. And selling still means talking.

When we see city governments being changed structurally in the face of years of acceptance, when we see campaigns for health funds succeed beyond hopes, when we see civic and social clubs spring up and grow strong where other clubs have failed, we may be sure that among other things, there has been some effective talking going on. When the planning staff gets together for conference, nothing else happens until all the proposals have been presented and *talked* over.

The salesman can't get much satisfaction from the fine points of a sales talk that doesn't sell; the campaigner will not delight long in the aesthetic qualities of the political speech that wins no votes; the civic-minded citizen is not so much concerned with the precision of his outlining and the beauty of his language as he is with the community response to his appeal. In all the possible situations in which the busy man may find himself called upon to speak he is trying to get certain results. Perhaps his purpose is to secure good will. Perhaps he simply wants to explain a process or impart valuable information. Maybe he is primarily interested in getting action from a group. Possibly he merely wants to entertain. He might be trying to gain understanding and support. Whatever his goal it must be clearly defined. The man who talks without purpose is a nuisance and ought to be discouraged. Those with something to say can be helped and should be helped. This book is intended for such people.

It is no accident that the book begins by stressing the attitudes the speaker brings to the speech. Much may be done in the way of improving diction, voice, and action in the speaker, but nothing will help the speaker to succeed if his attitudes toward the job are faulty. Hence the importance of sound concepts of the purposes and functions of the man who has the floor.

The exercises with each chapter are provided in recognition of the need for intelligent practice. Effective speech cannot be achieved through any magic formula — it can't be done in a week. It takes work. On the other hand anyone with something to say, the normal equipment for breathing and eating, and a little determination can become a competent speaker.

Acknowledgments

When one attempts to set down in some detail an approach to practical speech, the major problem is relatively simple. The accumulation of theory and practice that adds up to advice worth offering goes onto the paper rather smoothly. Not so easy is the task of identifying sources for acknowledgment. Through years of work in the field one acquires ideas and materials the sources of which escape him. More often than not a body of effective speech practice has been accumulated and validated by repetition — almost trial and error at times, and it becomes difficult to name names. Nevertheless, I have been strongly influenced by such men as Dr. James H. McBurney of Northwestern, Dr. Kenneth G. Hance at Michigan State University, and the late Dr. Lew Sarett.

Much credit must also go to former students whose success with the method has made the writing of such a book seem useful. The taught often supply new lines and suggest new methods. Most of us who teach have come away wiser from one or two well-remembered classes. Many friends in business and the professions have helped me to test techniques.

Certain people have contributed so directly and materially to the book that acknowledgment of their help is a pleasant duty here. Mr. Clarence Myers, President of New York Life; Mr. Roger Blough, Vice-President of United States Steel; Dr. W. Norman Wampler, Superintendent of Schools at Bellflower, California; and Mrs. Doris Schwinn Taylor of Muncie, Indiana, have all been kind enough to allow me to reprint their speeches in Part Four. The Sentinel Press has granted permission to reprint material from *Your Estate*. Dr. Lewis Toll, Chairman of the Business Education Department of Illinois State Normal University, has contributed directly to the section on *The Interview* in Part Four. Dr. Toll, Mr. John Tschantz of Caterpillar Company, Mr. George Harper of Bankers Life, and Mr. Kenneth Seitz of the New York Life Insurance Company have all examined various parts of this book and have made helpful suggestions. To Miss Marjorie Johnson of Bloomington, Illinois, a fortunate combination of speech expert and superior typist, I owe thanks for a fine job with the manuscript.

RALPH A. MICKEN

CONTENTS

PART 2 The Audience: *Who's Listening?*

PART 3 The Idea: *What's Being Talked About?*

PART 4   Typical Speech Situations

CONTENTS

Part One

The Speaker: Who's Talking?

THE SPEAKER'S ATTITUDE

TOWARD HIS JOB

"A man saying something to somebody"

Perhaps the first thing the prospective speaker should get straight is this: Important as he is in the situation, he is only a part of it. The listener is just as important as the speaker, and the *idea* may well be more important than either. We tend to personalize speechmaking out of all proportion. When the untrained man is confronted with a speaking job he tends to moan, "Who, me?" whereas the old hand asks, "What, and to whom?" If when you are asked to speak you quit feeling sorry for yourself and stop getting into your own private turmoil, you will have made a great step in the direction of good communication. You may feel that you are on the spot, but remember the idea and the audience are at *your* mercy too. Of course it matters who you are as a speaker, but it matters at least as much what you say and to whom you say it. The man who goes to work at once on what he will say and how he will say it will not have time to worry about himself. If he starts immediately to analyze his audience, he will have little time for self-torture.

After considering a few other concepts of the speaker, we will turn to a study of idea and audience. In the meantime re-

HANK BAEB

The Saturday Evening Post

"UNACCUSTOMED AS I AM TO PUBLIC SPEAKING . . ."

member this: With nothing to say and no one to listen we don't need a speaker.

"A man with a social obligation and a vocational need"

There is no end to the need for good speaking in our society. It must be evident to the reader that by far the larger part of his communication of ideas is by word of mouth. Whether he talks across a counter, from a living room chair, at an office desk, around a conference table, or from a platform — the average modern man must talk. Since speech is so important in vocational, civic, and social life, you have both an economic need and a social obligation to speak well. It can be put another way: you owe it to your product, your plans, and your proposals to present them well. A few years ago James H. McBurney, Dean of the School of Speech at Northwestern University and Moderator of the Reviewing Stand, attracted a good deal of attention with the observation that much of the advantage enjoyed by labor over management in public relations in recent times was due to labor's better method of presenting its case. The dean was impressed with the superiority of labor's speakers in getting across to the general public. There is a fairly common but mistaken notion that the man convinced of the rightness of his cause should merely stand calmly by, waiting for the public to see the truth — even feeling a little above getting out and vigorously talking for his ideas. It is imperative that the people with good ideas be especially good at expressing them.

"*A man who has made a deal*"

A good way to describe the speaker is to call him a man who has entered into a contract with an audience. To make a contract legally binding a consideration must be given by each party. The listeners have agreed on their part to sit comparatively still, to keep from interrupting, and to give their closest attention to the speaker. The speaker, in return, must meet certain obligations on his part; he must tell the listeners something worth while in a way easy to hear and understand. He must give them a reasonable return on the time and attention invested. The speaker who fails to keep his contract with his audience must expect the audience to feel cheated and to act accordingly. If the man across the conference table yawns, consults his watch openly — if the crowd out front shuffles and writhes audibly, or even starts its own little islands of discussion, the place to look for the trouble is in the speaker. People who have been taken in on deals may later become philosophical and charge it up to experience, but their first reaction is to express their resentment openly, and that is what the cheated listeners do.

"A man who knows what he is talking about"

The effective speaker must impress his listeners with the fact that he knows what he is talking about. Since the impact to be made by the speech is likely to be immediate and the modern speech is not very long, the speaker must make this impression of authoritativeness without taking time to tell all he knows. To put it bluntly, the speaker must reveal a thorough knowledge of his subject. It will be plain to speechmakers, of course, that the best way to seem to know is to know. Nevertheless, it will be worth while to exercise a little selective judgment in choosing examples and in wording one's information. Your detailed grasp of the subject can be strongly suggested in a half-hour speech; it can even be clearly indicated during a ten-minute talk; it cannot be exhaustively demonstrated. The thing for the speaker to do, then, is to pick out some one or two details which will make it seem probable to listeners that he speaks with authority. In a technological field this might be done through revealing acquaintance with some fairly obscure process connected with the particular branch of engineering under consideration. This is not a kind of low trickery, it is simply a matter of making the most of such knowledge as one possesses. Similarly, the salesman may do well to select deliberately certain structural qualities of his product to explain in detail when talking to a prospect.

Choice of language in which to express the detailed knowledge is also important in securing the impression of authoritativeness. It is not unusual for the speaker who is at ease with polysyllables to win scholarly prestige beyond that of others whose real knowledge might be much greater. The ideal, of course, is to set about educating the general listening public to the point where people will not be deceived by mere verbal facility. The present practical necessity, however, is what interests us here. If people are awed by imposing language at times, the man who must control audiences should be skilled in the use of such language. Finally the very physical presence of the speaker at the time of his speaking will contribute to his prestige in ways nonetheless real because they are hard to measure.

"A man of good character"

Aristotle wrote in his *Rhetoric* about twenty-two centuries ago, "It is more in keeping with true worth to show yourself as a man of honesty than as sharp in argument." And in so doing he put the finger on one of the profoundest truths of persuasive speaking. Of all the things the speaker must be to his audience, none is more important than this. People in this present world of multiple and confusing issues simply cannot arrive at the right answers to every question entirely on their own. Most of us know this; we know that if we are to take sides effectively in current controversies, reach intelligent decisions on many pressing problems, and take effective action where action is imperative, we must in a very real sense rely on the judgment and probity of those who lead us in controversy, problem solving, and final action. The average audience, then, has at the back of its mind the hope that it may get reliable leadership from the man to whom it has given the floor; it *wants* to trust the speaker — it needs to be able to trust him. The audience is listening and watching for signs that the speaker is a man to be trusted, and in our society it finds these evidences of good character in the *choices* the speaker makes on clearly recognized moral and ethical questions. The lawyer begins his defense of a thief with the observation that, of course, right-minded citizens (the lawyer and the audience) are able immediately to see the wrong in stealing, etc. . . . . He is setting up his own character as well as flattering the jury. The political orator tells how he fought through

7

innumerable obstacles on the way up, was too busy to have acquired the vices of liquor and tobacco, and learned too soon the values of money ever to squander the public funds. He relates incidents in his career when he was tempted by people who wanted to buy him. As the story goes on the listener nods wisely and thinks that here at last is a man who has met various moral and ethical crises in exemplary fashion and ought to be trusted in the office. The lawyer and the politician — and any other speaker who talks for keeps — have not achieved these effects accidentally. On the contrary, they have deliberately set up situations and confronted themselves with choices, in order that the listeners might be impressed with their honesty, sobriety, and overall strength of character.

The strong compulsion to seem to be in the right is perhaps best shown in our day by the Nazi group in Germany. It is fascinating to read the elaborate "white papers" published by the Hitler clique at the time of the invasion of Poland. In these papers the men who were about to perpetrate an act without the slightest moral justification in the eyes of the world nevertheless felt it worth while to put forth these rather ridiculous reports of threatened Polish aggression. They had to appear as the sinned against in this incident. The just and the unjust alike recognize the necessity of seeming to be people of good moral character to their audiences.

If you must secure a certain response from your hearer and that response depends to some extent upon the degree to which the hearer thinks he can rely upon your character, it becomes a part of your duty to provide for him strong reason for relying upon you. If you are inclined to be too proud, or if you are among those who feel that records speak for themselves, it is fair to remind you that your record may not have the chance to speak to the audience you now face. Records don't speak for themselves anyway, in the persuasive sense — they merely give speakers something to talk about. So when you get ready to make a speech, give real thought to the question, "Have I prepared myself to win the trust of this particular audience?"

"A man who is glad to be here"

There is nothing new in the idea that the effective speaker must seem to be well disposed toward his audience. Bored salesmen who sold were strictly a phenomenon of the war shortage period, and speakers who seem tired of it all are likely to be confined to classrooms and other centers of pressure without recourse. Since Aristotle it has been known that the manifestation of a friendly attitude toward the listeners is a *must* for persuasive speakers. The campaigning politician who starts all his speeches with "It gives me great pleasure to be here in your fine city" at every bowl-and-pitcher stop en route is on the right track. We incline to think he is being a bit obvious, perhaps, but even this shallow expression of good will wins more votes than it loses. The speaker must employ such actions and words as will suggest to the listeners that he is indeed happy to be talking to them. The smile is the best single means for conveying a feeling of good will. It is sound procedure to start every speech with a smile, and this goes for the speech in which you intend later to "roast 'em to a crisp," too.

Have no fear of being thought insincere — the psychologists are in no position as yet to tell us what part of *being* friendly lies in *acting* friendly, but the two cannot be separated completely. The speaker should not stop at such positive evidences of friendliness as the smile, however; he should be on guard against such actions and mannerisms as will suggest negatively. If your habitual thoughtful expression is a frown, better examine it carefully. It may look like just plain peevishness to your listener. If you react to the pressure of the speech situation by allowing your eyes to look everywhere except toward your audience that audience may interpret the absence of eye contact as evidence of a feeling of superiority. Similarly, the dead level of pitch to which many speakers retreat as a means of lessening the terror of facing an audience may be taken by the listeners as evidence of indifference.

The language may go far in conveying the impression of good will to the audience. We have already spoken of the over-worked phrase which may be used to tell the people you are happy to be before them. The trouble with such trite expressions is that they suggest a lack of spontaneous feeling; after all, the thinking listener will know that the words did not originate with the speaker; why should he suppose that the feeling comes from the speaker? To convey your own feelings it is important that you use your own style — your own language — your own stress.

"A man who knows how to communicate"

Viewed in another way the speaker may be thought of as a man who communicates orally with other men. This definition demands of the speaker that he have something to communicate and that he be able to communicate it at maximum efficiency. Crowds at track meets, thrilled by the smooth work of winning relay teams, are often unaware of the long practice involved in developing skill at passing the baton. The runner who cannot hand along the baton may easily lose the race for a potentially faster team. Speakers must be able to pass ideas along smoothly. There are several ways of looking at the speaker as a communicator. Some think the stress should be put on content. These conceive of the speaker primarily as someone with an idea worth communicating. They are prone to leave matters of delivery to chance; they show great faith in the power of ideas to triumph over their environment — physical, verbal, and vocal.

Others feel that the emphasis should all be placed on the manner of speaking. Such people sometimes forget the importance of having something to say and concentrate on high-flown and trite expressions, beautiful gestures, and the cultivation of a silver-toned voice. It is not necessary, however, to take sides in this controversy. The speaker will do well to divide his efforts between content and delivery as his special needs indicate. It is only fair, however, to inject here the observation that this book has deliberately put the stress on the *way to speak*, and has left most of the work on the *way to think* to such other books as have very probably already taken care of that technique for most of the readers.

"A man who is a psychologist"

The good speaker must be a psychologist. After all, speaking is largely a matter of stimulus and response. Communication involves the application of certain auditory and visual stimuli so that the response is accurate understanding. Persuasion is a problem in securing certain responses in the form of attitudes and actions, and these responses depend upon the use of selected emotional stimuli calculated to get these reactions.

What is more, the speaker must understand and employ suggestion. In spite of himself the man before the audience is suggesting — either negatively or positively. The decisive point is that he understand suggestion so that while he talks he will be suggesting positively and to his advantage. This involves a wide range of possibilities.

How he looks, for examples: A sloppy, ill-dressed man will not suggest incisive character or clear thinking.

How he uses his voice: A good idea expressed in excellent language can be damaged by a weak, hesitant voice. A noisy, excited delivery may shake the listeners' confidence in a speaker who has really fine things to say.

How he chooses his words: Powerful ideas, potentially strong appeals may be muffled or weakened if put into words that suggest vagueness and uncertainty. Remember the service station attendant who didn't ask "How much?" but "Fill 'er up?" He now says "Ethyl?"

How he arranges his ideas: Most speakers come up with a few good ideas in an hour's talking. These may lose half their impact if they are not arranged so that they march powerfully to the conclusion desired. An example will help here. During a recent campaign a speaker was presenting an appeal for the sup-

11

port of a candidate for the office of county attorney. The candidate's qualifications included intelligence, integrity, training, and experience. Note, however, how they gain by the order in which they were presented: First, our candidate is a man of high native intelligence. Second, but more than that, he has had the best legal education. Third, in addition he has had five years of valuable experience in the courts. Fourth, but most important of all, his record and reputation make it clear that he is a man of the highest integrity.

"A man who often speaks as a member of a group"

Much stress is now put upon conference. The busy man will probably have more occasion to speak as part of a group than from the platform. What are some of the implications of this kind of speaking? Naturally the actual speaking time will be relatively short. Even when you are the only speaker on more-or-less formal occasions long speeches are rarely in order. In the discussion long-winded statements and little orations are never good. The discussant therefore will work for conciseness, exactness, and brevity. If he has much to say, he may enter the discussion at several points and thus get everything said without taking over for long periods.

The style will be less formal, more conversational; the organization less tight. This does not mean, however, that discussion talk should be sloppy, fragmented, and ill-organized. If there is a danger in the present trend toward conference it lies right here. I have heard a number of people make the comment, "Oh, if it's just a discussion I can get by." Actually good communication is just as important in group talking as it is in single speaker situations. Incisive utterance, suggestive language, and clear thinking should always characterize speech if it is to be effective.

Since exhaustive treatment of the subject is no longer required of the individual, some people think that discussion relieves them of the need for thorough study of the subject. Of course, the member will take away something new from the group meeting, but this in no way releases him from the duty of bringing all the information and thought that he can to the meeting.

Groups usually get together to seek agreement by talking things over. This calls for an open-minded attitude on the part of each member. Even if you have a preconceived notion as to what the group ought to think, you will do well not to come to meeting without the intention of giving everyone a hearing.

The conference is usually called for the purpose of finding out or deciding. This means that the participant is both a listener and a talker; he is both information-giver and informed.

An insurance man in an evening class once told me that what he really needed was not only a course in how to speak but also a few lessons in when to keep quiet. Group discussion, more than any other speech situation, puts a premium upon frequent busy silences on the part of the participant. What you say when you speak is bound to be more valuable if you have been listening. The times when you aren't speaking should never seem to be frustrating and unproductive interludes to be endured until you can get the floor again. How well do you listen?

EXERCISES

Now that we have considered the question of what the speaker should be, it is time to turn to the tasks of self-analysis. What equipment do you bring to the job? What are your strong points? What things about you are likely to need working over and correction before you can speak effectively?

The following Evaluation Questionnaire should help you get a line on your strengths and your needs. Ask several people who know you to fill it out. Tell them they don't need to sign it; urge them to be frank. Fill out one for yourself.

Personal Persuasiveness Evaluation

Answer yes, no, or x (no impression).

Voice

_____ Is the voice clear?
_____ Is it loud enough?
_____ Is it too fast?
_____ Is it too slow?
_____ Is it smooth and easy?
_____ Are there many "ahs"?
_____ Is it conversational?
_____ Is the voice noisy?
_____ Is the voice monotonous?
_____ Is the voice shrill?
_____ Does the voice stress the points?
_____ Do you like to listen to the voice?

How would you rate this person as to total voice impression?
Strong _____ Adequate _____ Fair _____ Inadequate _____ Definitely weak _____

Appearance

_____ Are his clothes in good taste?
_____ Are the clothes conservative?
_____ Are the clothes zooty? Eccentric?
_____ Is the dress sloppy?
_____ Is the posture good?
_____ Is the person relaxed?
_____ Is he stiff and overformal?
_____ Does he suggest confidence?
_____ Are there many gestures?
_____ Are there many facial expressions?
_____ Are the actions vigorous? Energetic?
_____ Are there any distracting mannerisms?
_____ Does the speaker seem to be talking right to you?
_____ Does he seem embarrassed? Apologetic?
_____ Does he seem overbearing? Overconfident?
_____ Does the speaker seem interested?

14

How would you rate this person as to total appearance impression?
Strong _____ Adequate _____ Fair _____ Inadequate _____ Definitely weak _____

Language
_____ Does the speaker have enough words?
_____ Does he seem to prefer formal language?
_____ Does he use words correctly?
_____ Are his words fresh and interesting?
_____ Does he use lively figures of speech?
_____ Does he use slang?
_____ Is the slang helpful?
_____ Is his grammar satisfactory?
_____ Does he have pet expressions?
_____ Does he use much worn-out language?
_____ Does he use any offensive language?
_____ Does he tend to repeat himself?

How would you rate this person as to total language impression?
Strong _____ Adequate _____ Fair _____ Inadequate _____ Definitely weak _____

Ideas
_____ Does the speaker have many ideas?
_____ Does he support the ideas with examples?
_____ Does he have quotations from authorities?
_____ Does he use convincing statistics?
_____ Does he make sense — are his ideas logical?
_____ Is his thinking well organized?
_____ Is it scattered — poorly organized?
_____ Is it easy to follow his reasoning?
_____ Are his ideas interesting?

How would you rate this person as to ideas?
Strong _____ Adequate _____ Fair _____ Inadequate _____ Definitely weak _____

Some of your findings will probably surprise you. Among those to whom I have assigned this questionnaire in the past I recall especially a young salesman who was horrified to discover that some people thought of him as sporty — a drinker and smoker. To a rare smoker and total abstainer this was a blow.

A well-established manager who thought himself affable and friendly was tabbed as cold and hardboiled. A teacher who thought himself well dressed was puzzled to find that he gave the impression of being "zooty" and "a kind of cat."

On the other side I have seen men who thought their voice and appearance bad, reassured by favorable responses.

Once you have collected these impressions, look for evidences of weakness and strength. Work to eliminate the former and utilize the latter. Many people react to criticism by becoming angry or discouraged. This of course will do you no good. Intelligent work on the results should help you as a speaker.

DELIVERING THE SPEECH

"Disposing of the body"

In the "whodunit" story, one of the toughest problems for the murderer is that of disposing of the body. The problem is only slightly less troublesome for the man who intends to commit speech. Many a person with something to say has found to his sorrow that he'd have been better off had he been able to leave himself at home. For a while it seemed that the radio would provide an escape for the speaker whose physical presence proved an almost insuperable obstacle to communication, but television will soon have removed even that haven. It is safe to say that the speaker must bring himself along whenever he goes speaking. The only question worth considering here is what to do about it. There are three ways of handling the problem: One may let his presence interfere with the communication of ideas and the expression of feelings, one may try simply to use the body as a kind of flesh and blood loud-speaker stand, or one may employ the body actively to aid in the communication.

The first of these methods has one advantage — it takes no practice. The speaker simply lurches, prances, or slinks to the platform, stands like a wading bird, clings frantically to the table, or paces madly across the confines of the platform like the leading character in a zoo. He flaps his arms like fins, or makes

17

abortive little twitches of the hands without relinquishing his grip on the reading stand; he rolls and unrolls his notes or his necktie, swallows like an ostrich with an orange, and runs his finger around the inside of his collar. What is even worse, he may seem to lapse into a semiconscious state, escaping from the pain of the speech situation by inducing a kind of overall abstraction through staring wistfully at all windows and exits, coyly at his feet, and prayerfully overhead. In this technique the speaker employs his actions to deny vigorously the importance of anything he may say.

The second possibility, that of making oneself a kind of human loud-speaker, does take considerable discipline. The speaker stands with the weight of the body evenly distributed on the balls of the feet, the hands firmly at the sides, and the face directed toward the audience. The idea here is that, since he can't leave his physical presence at home, the speaker is going to keep everything under control. There is only one thing wrong with this approach — it won't work. The listener (and looker) hears the stirring words, the exciting facts issuing from the immobile body and he just can't believe it. It isn't natural. People simply don't act that way. The very absence of bodily action is almost as distracting as awkward, ill-motivated movement.

The third method remains. If nervous, pointless action is bad, and absolute restraint is neither possible nor desirable, then the habit of using bodily action to further the ideas and feelings of the speaker is the goal to be sought. What can be done about it?

As a starter, let's state a principle: Any action which contributes to the communication of the idea or the expression of the feeling is good. Let's put it negatively: Any action which interferes with the communication of the idea or the expression of the feeling is bad. This principle brings hope and a warning. It means that the speaker who has been talking at reduced efficiency and with his voice only may look for improvement in the use of motivated action, that he may channel off the nervous tensions which have been producing distracting action into facial expressions, gestures, and posture which will fortify the words he utters. On the other hand, it should warn the elocutionary, dramatic type whose actions are too apparently studied and practiced that those actions are likely to be observed for their own sake and not as a part of the idea.

"Gesture and posture"

A glance at the writings of any speech teacher in the post-elocutionary period will reveal the presence of a real difficulty in the teaching of bodily action. We don't want to suggest to the speaker that he learn certain fixed gestures. We want to leave no doubt that the only worth-while actions are those which arise from the need of the speaker to communicate "all over" as it were, and yet we know that, left to themselves, most speakers, while showing unmistakable signs of wanting to use gestures, simply can't get them out. In other words, the unpracticed speaker can't use gestures and actions which will contribute to communication. The answer seems to be this: The effective use of gesture must be acquired through practice. It seems likely that some few people upon learning the clenched-fist movement will forever after seem stagey in making this gesture; most people will discover, rather, that a little practice on it gives inevitability to such bodily movement as they find themselves making in moments of great anger or determination. It may be that ducks thrown in the water find themselves able to swim, but apparently the function of communication is by no means so basic. What we are after in our gesturing is the *effect* of inevitability. This can best be achieved through deliberate practice. Get before a mirror and find out how you look to your audience.

There are many ways of classifying and labeling gestures of the hand and arm, but for our purposes we may divide them into descriptive and formal. The descriptive gestures include use of the index finger to point things out, the use of the hands to show the length of the big one that got away, and gestures indicating the manipulation of various things. It is futile to list these gestures since the possibilities are almost unlimited. Perhaps the best way to indicate how important such gestures may be is to watch the activities of people while they are trying to describe how to play a violin. The only advice worth giving here is that you use descriptive gestures as often as you feel impelled. Perhaps it is only fair to warn the speaker of the inaccuracies, or at least the irregularities, of visual perception. Therefore, it would be well to make your descriptive gestures as unmistakable as it is possible to make them for all observers. You might, of course, find yourself in the position of the fisherman just returned from the lakes. In his desire to make the most of his accomplishments with rod and reel, he used the following device. With skeptical friends he started the length of the fish at about three feet and, keeping an eye on his listener, he brought his hands closer together until he read acceptance on the skeptic's face. With sympathetic or gullible friends, he reversed the procedure, starting with his hands three feet apart and moving them away from each other until his listeners showed doubt. This is the way to get the most out of a fish or a gesture.

Formal gestures include all those which come to the speaker in his effort to vivify and intensify ideas and feelings. Some of these must have been descriptive originally. For example, the index gesture which one uses in saying to an audience of five hundred people, "This is your responsibility," must have sprung originally from the simple pointing gesture. And the clenched-fist gesture, indicating determination and aggressiveness bears some resemblance to a completed uppercut, pugilistically speaking. The so-called soothing gesture, used in telling a large audience to go slow or take it easy, has some kinship to a pat on the head. To go farther, any gesture which might accompany the statement, "Let us aid these people; let us lift them out of their misery," would find the hands turned fingers upward in a literally lifting position.

Let us get this straight. This is not intended as a return to studied elocution. There are usually many ways of making the

20

formal gesture, whether it be didactic, clenched-fist, index-finger, or casting-aside, and we do not advocate just one way of making each of these. Nevertheless, if the hand is held like a paddle or a cleaver, if the arms are straight at the elbow and the clenched-fist gesture resembles a straight left by Joe Louis, the effect is not good. If the timing is bad, so that the gesture hits too long before or too long after the word to be stressed, the effect is ludicrous. Years of experience with speakers have convinced the writer that graceful and effective gestures do not spring full-blown from earnest speaking. Carefully observed practice of bodily action is the only means of insuring effective bodily action. Remember, by effective bodily action we mean any action of hand, arm, or eyebrow which contributes to the communication of the idea or feeling, whether the contribution be made to the speaker communicating or to the audience receiving the idea.

"Eye contact"

In looking over what the speaker does, and evaluating it, a prominent place must be given to what is perhaps best described as eye contact. It is quite evident that a man who stands before a group of people to address them should realize the importance of talking, not in front of them, at them, or past them, but *to* them. For better or worse, the average listener feels that he is being talked to only when he is being looked at. When he can see the speaker, this listener is likely to be distracted if the speaker does not look directly at his audience while talking to it. This works the other way too; the speaker feels that he is communicating more directly with people when he looks at them. This direct glance was characteristic of the great orator Robert G. Ingersoll. Albert Beveridge, writing about Ingersoll, says, "He came to the front of the platform in a most natural manner, and looking us in the eye in a friendly fashion, began to talk to us as if he were conversing with each of us personally."

The need for eye contact is pointed up pretty vividly on

TV. So often we are treated to the spectacle of some otherwise perfectly normal celebrity staring blankly from the screen. The uncomfortable gentleman has not been hit on the head with a blunt instrument — he is merely struggling with a teleprompter and can't focus on audience and lines simultaneously.

A good way to secure eye contact if you are having trouble is to pick out individuals seated at intervals across the front of your audience. Start talking to someone at the extreme left and move the glance to the next person in order at the right until you have spoken directly to the whole audience. This will keep you from ignoring parts of your audience. Return in the same stages from right to left. Don't go too fast. You don't want to give the effect of a spectator at a tennis match. After a few sessions of this arbitrary procedure you will find yourself acquiring the habit of eye contact. At a large business session in Lincoln, Nebraska, a few years ago I happened to be seated near a group of young men who were in opposition to the resolution under discussion. Their spokesman rose repeatedly to gain recognition from the presiding officer. As others were recognized and had their say and he was still ignored the frustrated member started to mutter about walking out with his delegation, when suddenly one of the group made an interesting discovery. Our chairman had his glance fixed on the left side of the room all of the time. He had acquired this habit unconsciously, of course, but it effectively cut out everyone to his right. The group hurried their spokesman to the other side of the house where he was recognized almost immediately and was thus able to enter debate. This was an extreme case but you had better check yourself to see if perhaps you have a favorite direction that makes some of your listeners feel left out.

For man-to-man conferences, of course, this sort of thing can be overdone. We have all been subjected to the serpent-and-rabbit technique of certain salesmen and promoters who have confronted us nose to nose and fixed us with a glassy stare. The apparent intent here is to hypnotize the prospect into a state of acceptance or perhaps to render his position so obnoxious that he will agree to anything to escape. As a matter of fact, it is sound advice for the conferee to glance away occasionally from the man across the table and to return at intervals with a frank, friendly, and interested look to the eye of the listener.

"Nervous mannerisms"

We should not leave the subject of bodily action without some reference to the habit that many speakers have of fussing with a favorite key, sliding a pen or pencil through the fingers, tracing patterns on the speakers' stand with the finger tips or rolling up notes. These practices quite evidently provide psychological crutches for the speaker; they are just as evidently distracters for the audience. The best advice is to rid yourself of such mannerisms if it is at all feasible, especially if the activity takes a form which does the audience more harm in the way of diverted attention than it does the speaker good in the way of a nervous outlet. A good many years ago there was a superintendent of schools in a certain western city who never spoke in public without first fishing a ring of keys from his pocket and taking a firm grip upon one of the keys. The habit attracted the attention of several young men who eventually made away with the key ring and completely demoralized the poor administrator. The chances are that if you have developed the habit of depending upon some such device you should wean yourself away from it as soon as possible. Check yourself carefully, or better yet get a friend to check you for such quirks.

"Stage fright and doing what comes naturally"

It is popular nowadays to avoid any mention of the phenomenon of stage fright, on the theory that a positive approach to the problem may best be made by denying its existence. The truth of the matter is that the symptoms and manifestations which we group under the term "stage fright" are, taken separately, examples of the unmotivated bodily action we spoke of earlier in

23

this chapter. Because the speech situation is not a "natural" one, certain tensions are built up in the speaker, and these are released in twitchings, clumsy swallowings, vocalized stops, eye rollings, and robot movements. It is wise to expect these symptoms. They are inevitable for most of us unless we do something about them. The thing to do is to channel the tensions into controlled and motivated actions which will not only release the tension but will contribute to the communication of the idea being expressed. Of course frequent experiences in the speech situation will eventually produce a modification of the strain. Practice in speaking is basic in all phases of speech, but heroic repetition of the speech experience is of no use at all unless good habits are going to result. At this point gestures and facial expressions come in again. Strong, positively suggestive action aids the listener; it will do as much for the speaker who employs it. Psychologists are at present not sure about the part that the outward evidences of a feeling play in the feeling, but it seems clear that these outward symptoms of an emotion produce the emotion as often as they are produced by the emotion. If you haven't put to use before the practice of frowning, clenching the fists, and gritting the teeth to induce wrath and determination, try doing these things the next time you wish to convey these feelings before an audience.

Now a few words on the naturalistic approach to public speaking. Since Whately, probably a poor speaker in his own right, began to preach the doctrine that speech should flow in adequate forms from the man with soundly organized and worthwhile ideas, the naturalists in speech have remained prominent. Lest someone has convinced you that doing what comes naturally is effective public speaking, let's look into the claims of such people. They tell you that if you have a fine idea and a strong desire to put it across you can speak effectively; that if you burn with zeal, or even anger, then you can take the floor and hold your audience spellbound. "Does the man whose house is burning need a course in speech to express the alarm?" they ask. The answer is that he probably does not, but a man can scarcely set fire to his house every time he wants to get in the mood for effective communication. Let us picture a situation dear to the hearts of the "naturalists." A man has found the solution to a serious problem in which he knows his listeners are vitally interested. Being a public-spirited person, he is desperately eager to tell his good news to these people — but he speaks only English and the crowd understands only French. He can't communicate at all. He wants to, he ought to, he simply can't. One may say, of course, that this is a special situation in which a purely mechanical obstacle renders effective communication impossible, and so it is. So are the situations in which the speaker, equally eager to tell something equally worth telling, doesn't get across because of failure to use adequate language or failure to speak loudly enough to be heard, clearly enough to be understood, or movingly enough to be listened to.

In summary, the public speaker who would control the responses of his listeners must examine his appearance and actions before those listeners with a view to making his physical presence a positive aid to communication. He should deliberately work to acquire ease in gesture, posture, and facial expression. Above all he should make use of bodily action; he should not allow himself to be restrained, stiff, and unnatural from the mistaken idea that vigorous action is undignified. Forceful and "inevitable" movements will aid the speaker and the listener equally. There is no excuse for you as a speaker to limp along without them.

"Clothes can make the difference"

What about the clothes you wear? In an age that is beginning to challenge cuffs on trousers, lapels on coats, neckties, and polished shoes this is a difficult problem. But even if we take into account Bermuda shorts and tropical shirts, we must still recommend "conservative" as the word for conference, interview, and small informal group dress. We will go farther and say "formal" for the big occasion and its speaker. Conservative and formal have, of course, both slipped a notch or two in recent years. Nevertheless they still mean a coat, a light shirt, necktie, and neat shoes for all speech situations, and white shirt, dark tie, dark suit (perhaps a tuxedo) for the larger occasions. I know the trend and fear it. No one will be less surprised than the writer if in a decade or less this insistence upon some formality in dress should make amusing reading. These recommendations still stand. Erratic dress will distract and disturb more people than it will impress, among those whose attention you covet.

Women will, of course, work for the tailored look. Heels and hose, and I hope a suit. This need not be dark but it should be tailored. I hesitate to prescribe for hair, but I will go this far — it ought to look "contained." If there are earrings they should be small and close to the head. In short, the woman speaker's appearance should be such that having looked the audience will remain willing to listen.

"Efficient use of the voice"

People who teach speech are often told wistfully by students that it's too bad we can't all be silver-tongued orators. The implication is that there is a certain voice the possession of which will assure speaking success to its possessor, and that all the people who lack that kind of voice have two strikes on them in the matter of oral communication. This is not true, of course. As a matter of fact, there are almost as many potentially effective speaking voices as there are speakers. There are only three requirements for a satisfactory speaking voice. First, it must be loud enough to be heard; second, it must be clear enough to be understood; third, it must be pleasant enough to be endured.

"Loud enough"

As to just how loud is loud enough, the speaker himself must decide. The necessary volume will be determined by the size and acoustical qualities of the room, the amount of interference from outside noises, the use of a public address system, perhaps even the age of the listeners. The careful speaker will make an advance check on the place where he is to speak. If possible have a listener go to each area of the auditorium and test reception of your voice. Check on the necessity for public address equipment, and on the effectiveness of such equipment as is supplied. It is well to remember that the best of current microphones are likely to be troublesome to the speaker, chaining him as they do to a certain area of movement and gesture. All that may be said for such devices is that it is better to use them than not to be heard. Since the average auditorium is built and equipped with little or no regard to acoustics, anyone who has any reason to expect that he might be called upon to address large audiences should work before a microphone from time to time until the situation is no longer distracting to him. As a rule, however, the speaking will be done in places where it is entirely possible for the average voice to provide sufficient volume, if attention is given to the specific needs of the room. In small lecture halls, conference rooms, classrooms or courtrooms the speaker need simply make more noise if he is to be heard. Partly from shyness and partly from a mistaken notion of dignity, many people keep their voices muffled and subdued whenever they stand before listeners. It is probably advisable for the average person to talk a little louder than seems right to him whenever he speaks before a group. If the speaker has as his goal the communication of ideas and the expression of feelings, certainly he must be heard, and if one had to choose between being too loud or not loud enough he should have to vote for too loud.

Such a choice isn't necessary, however. For the average audience in the average place it is possible to make the adjustment of volume until it is neither too loud nor too weak, but just right. Good advice here is to watch your listeners as you speak. Turn on more force when the folks in the far corners start cupping their hands behind their ears or taking on the strained facial expression that you yourself have often used when struggling to hear someone. Cut down a bit if the people up

27

close begin to show irritation and restlessness. The more seasoned you become the greater the danger that you will neglect the "enough" in "loud enough" and will start shouting at little audiences of fifteen or twenty and orating at interviewers. It is disconcerting but helpful to catch yourself shouting fairly early in your speaking career. Although it is true that it is better to bellow than to mumble, there is no doubt that the person who speaks noisily is providing a distracting element which can defeat attention almost as effectively as failure to be heard at all.

"Clear enough"

But it is not enough that your voice be loud enough to be heard; it must also be clear enough to be understood. Distinctness of articulation is probably (not pronounced "prolly") the most important characteristic of speech. For our purposes articulation may be thought of as having to do with the consonants in the alphabet. Man is hardly distinguished for his vowels. Most of the other mammals do all the vowels, and some of them do certain vowels a great deal better than man. What makes our system of oral communication distinctive is the set of adjustments we make in the speech mechanism before, during, and after the vowel sound. Taking the opening words of the *Gettysburg Address*, for example, and stripping them of their consonant sets we get "oh oh uh eh eh ee uh oh." These sounds don't mean much until the distinguishing consonants are added, and then they become "Fourscore and seven years ago." Yet frequently the listener is bombarded with a series of grunts, whoops, and coughs while some speaker tries to get ideas across without giving proper attention to distinctness of utterance. Many speakers achieve meaningless burbles of sound because they are making sure of being loud enough to be heard without taking care of being clear enough to be understood.

Indistinctness most frequently results from failure to stress or fully form end consonants. Overpreciseness in everyday talking is, of course, an affectation more likely to be tolerated in an

English teacher than in most of us. If it impinges on our awareness it is poor speech technique. Nevertheless the absolute necessity that the public speaker be understood makes it advisable
that he lean over backward a bit in precision of utterance while
on the platform. It is better that the listener wonder why you
said a thing so precisely, than that he wonder what you said.

"Listenable enough"

When we enter into a consideration of the qualities that
make a voice attractive or "listenable" we are on dangerous
ground. After all, the majority of those who heard Lincoln
seem to have agreed that his voice was almost as unprepossessing
as his appearance. It was called high-pitched, squeaky, and
nasal. Yet it is possible that in Honest Abe these very qualities
intensified his appeal to listeners. Certainly from the standpoint
of the voice perfectionists, Winston Churchill's rather mushy
and flat tones leave a great deal to be desired, yet for Churchill
the voice seems no particular handicap. What is more important,
it is unlikely that the unlovely qualities of the great Britisher's
voice greatly disturb his listeners, unless they be speech experts.
Similarly it may be pointed out that a voice so often given the
accolade by the voice authorities as that of Franklin Roosevelt
still managed to sound oily and insincere to many folks, not all
of whom voted the Republican ticket. It is hazardous to attempt an arbitrary list of voice characteristics as being bad. Still,
one may mention at least four which almost always reduce the
"listenability" of the speaker. First of these is shrillness. This
strained quality in the voice strongly suggests discomfort in the
speaker and makes the audience correspondingly uncomfortable.
It seems to be a part of the overall reaction of earnestness and
excitement that the voice should go up. The speaker should
simply remind himself from time to time to relax a bit. Shrill
voices belong to people who allow their voices to go up at excited moments and then forget to bring them down afterward.

A second quality which, when present in excess, makes the

voice hard to listen to, is nasality. If this is due to some chronic stoppage in the nasal passages, it must be treated by doctors. If, as is more often true, the nasal quality comes from the habit of directing sounds into but not through the nasal passages, it simply calls for a supplanting of the habit of misdirecting the sounds you are nasalizing. A time-honored means for checking on your habit of nasalizing is that of saying the alphabet while holding the nostrils tightly shut. If direction is correct only "m" and "n" should be interfered with in this process.

The third and most serious interference with listenability is the habit of speaking in a monotone. There is a definite tendency for the unpracticed speaker to erect barriers between himself and his audience. He does this in order to reduce the pressure of the speech situation. The most effective of these barriers is the monotonous voice. The speaker gets on one dead level of pitch and goes on and on until he has knocked himself out and reduced the listeners to a state bordering upon sleep. In this situation the man who has the floor can mumble on for hours without feeling any of the pain of direct audience contact. The only flaw in the technique is that somnolent listeners cannot attend well to half-stunned talkers, and no useful purpose is being served.

It is not at all unusual to hear a man who speaks without variety of pitch and stress trying to get vital information across to an audience while his deadening manner of speech makes it almost impossible for the listeners to follow. No college professor is more heartily detested than the one who drones out his lectures in a manner that balks attention and then cracks down on any failure to get complete notes. If the world's lullabies have not been written on an erroneous assumption, it is damaging to communication to speak in a repetitive tone. The best way to fight against this mannerism is to speak and read into a recording device, and play it back for study and correction. Perhaps, too, it will be helpful to remember that, as a rule, the level of voice rises as the rate is accelerated, and drops as the pace is slowed.

A fourth enemy to enjoyable listening is the affected voice. This seems sometimes to be the peculiar affliction of pulpit orators, although it is by no means confined to clergymen. The affected manner of speaking goes along with trite and pompous language, magnificent gestures, and generally overdone actions. On the several occasions when I have brought myself to comment on this pulpit manner, the preachers have responded that they had a definite feeling the congregation wanted to hear them talk this way — expected to hear rolling tones and pious notes on Sunday along with the church bells. To put it mildly, this belief seems to be held on insufficient evidence. Occasionally lawyers, too, are guilty of a special jury manner accomplished through loud barkings and vibrating jowls. I have never heard it claimed, however, that juries also expect this of lawyers as part of the courtroom atmosphere. As a matter of fact, some people, regardless of vocation, seem to have picked up the notion that a certain affectation of tone and manner is an essential part of public speaking.

"Trough noises"

This seems to be a good point at which to consider what is perhaps the most pervasive sin of human utterance — "the trough noise." The audience has settled back, ready to be informed, entertained, impressed, or convinced. The speaker strides forth to the platform, puts his notes firmly on the table before him; fixes his listeners with his eye; opens his mouth; and says, "Uh-h-h." To say the least, this is somewhat of a letdown for the listener who, although he may have had little notion what the speaker was going to discuss, certainly had a right to expect more than this. What is a great deal worse is that the speaker may go on with a series of weird grunts and wheezes throughout the whole speech. It is not unusual for some speakers to use close to twenty per cent of their speaking time in the utterance of these unintelligible noises. We have already referred to the agreement which exists between the speaker and his audience; any listener has a right to expect more than a collection of "ahs" and "ers" from the speaker to whom he has surrendered his time.

The three main objections to "trough noises" in public speaking are these: (1) from the aesthetic standpoint, they render speech hideous; (2) they are time-wasting since communication is certainly not going on during vocalized stops; and (3) they are a primary source of negative suggestion. Lack of incisiveness, vagueness and tentativeness, lack of authoritativeness, are all impressed upon the listener when the speaker seems unable to go from one word to another without a lot of hemming and hawing. The reasons for these vocalized stops are several. One of them has to do with the relative speed of the passage of time as estimated by the speaker and the listener. To the former, the interim between words during extemporization may seem almost endless. He feels that he is standing mute and stupid for an embarrassingly long time waiting for the next word to come; and speakers abhor an interim of silence almost as much as nature was once thought to abhor a vacuum. What does the anxious speaker do about it? That's easy. He simply fills in the gaps with meaningless sounds. It may even be that some people have reached the strange conclusion that all this business of "ahs" and "ers" gives a judicious and deliberative flavor to speech. If, however, we remember that the main purpose of speech is communication, and judge the "trough noise" on the basis of its communicative value, we will find no justification for it whatever.

It is not particularly difficult to break the habit. It is simply a matter of reminding yourself, whenever you arise to speak, that you should do nothing at all in the places where you are now making these animal noises. It will be helpful too, if you tend to dread even momentary silence on the platform, for you to remember that time is not passing as rapidly for your listeners as it seems to be for you. In any event, meaningless sounds provide very little entertainment during the wait.

"Pitch and rate can influence thought and feeling"

Technically pitch rises as the frequency of the vibration of the vocal folds increases. Pitch drops as frequency drops. These vocal folds are located in the larynx (Adam's apple) in the throat. Fortunately this bit of scientific information isn't needed by the average person in his efforts to control pitch. You can talk at a higher or lower pitch by simply trying or willing yourself to do so. Even the range you achieve isn't as important in speech as it would be in singing. As long as you can make the voice vary from high to low so that the variations can be heard easily you have nothing to worry about. On the chance that your voice will work upward during a long speech and stay high, it is wise to pause from time to time and start out on a corrected pitch when you introduce new ideas.

Speed is, of course, simply the rate at which you speak. You can control this pretty much as you wish to if you are the average person. Speed usually varies somewhat along with pitch and in a consistent pattern: fast rate — high pitch; slow rate — low pitch. It might help you to know this when you are working for voice control in the exercises. The time it takes to utter a passage can be controlled either by shortening or lengthening the intervals between words or by holding the sounds themselves longer within the words.

For better or worse we associate certain pitch-rate patterns with certain moods and temperament. High pitch and high speed suggest excitement, nervousness, joy, anger, anxiety; the low-slow combination suggests calm, thoughtfulness, sorrow, peace, even stolid indifference.

If your voice is disturbingly high or unnaturally slow, don't give up without a struggle. If practice of the lower tones and discipline in rate don't seem to help you it is still likely that there is a speech correctionist nearby who can aid you with specialized diagnosis and treatment.

EXERCISES

1. *Gestures*

For purposes of practice before your mirror, work out bodily action, both facial expression and gesture for the following sentences.

(1) This is your responsibility; you cannot escape it.

(2) There is nothing that management can do about this.

(3) I suggest that we work day and night for the improvement of this community.

(4) Pause, if you will, for just a moment; consider the consequences of the course you propose to adopt.

(5) The people of poverty-stricken Asia need your help. What are you ready to do about it?

(6) Let us forget old quarrels. Let us put them behind us and work together from here on.

(7) There are two ways to look at the problem: Obviously better education will be more expensive; equally obviously some limit must be put to public expenditures.

2. *Stress*

Stress is one of the special advantages of speech. Hitting the right words with more force will serve to emphasize them and thus point up their significance. Stress is achieved by simply turning on more volume, shifting pitch and slowing speed. It is usually best accomplished without violent changes in pitch, volume, or rate. Work with the following expressions. Pick out different words for stress each time you read a passage. Experiment with louder volume, change of voice level, and speed. Try them one at a time or in combination. Record several readings of each sentence and play back for checking purposes.

(1) Why did he do it? (Read this four times, stressing first "why," then "did," etc. Notice how the meaning is affected.)

(2) If I remember rightly, and I think I do, the letter called for a statement of our overall policy.

(3) He was never fair, never careful, and always a little less than completely honest, but I suppose we shouldn't set ourselves up as judges.

(4) It has always been helpful to have security; security with profit is even better.

(5) We can't take this course of action unless we are prepared to go the whole way. Are we ready for that?

(6) No, I don't think I'd like to do that.

(7) Where did Smith get that idea?

(8) Slowly, one at a time, and with no panic they left the building.

(9) To get things done do them, not later, but now.

3. *Pitch and rate*

Record your reading of the following passages. Try a fast rate on all of them the first time. Then a slow rate. After that try for maximum effect on each phrase by experimenting until you have the most meaningful rate and pitch. Note how some sentences call for definite help that only the voice can give.

(1) No! They couldn't have given it to him.

(2) Let's get this work done quickly. Perhaps later, when we have time we can slow up.

(3) He ran to the corner, peeked around, and seeing the way clear, jumped into his car and took off like a jet pilot.

(4) The birthrate has increased at an amazing pace — 11 per cent in ten years. Just what should we gather from this trend?

(5) Have you never longed for a calm time by the sea or in the far, still woods? No nagging rush, no day and night grind of unrelenting pressure. Just sleepy peace.

(6) Twenty-five points in one game! I told you he was a fine prospect.

(7) Now let's see; we have a long way to go and all the time in the world to get there.

(8) You may protest, you may say you're sick to death of heavy taxes, but what are you willing to do about it? Do you really believe, down deep, that anything will be done about them?

4. *Voice and gesture work together*

Be sure that you are getting the most out of your remarks by using your voice and gesture at maximum efficiency.

Take the sentences we have already used for gesture and point them up now with voice as well as action.

(1) This is your responsibility; you cannot escape it.

> Is "this" the main thing? If so hit it: "*This* is your responsibility";
>
> Has there been some doubt? If so hit "is": "This *is* your responsibility";
>
> Is the fact that it's yours paramount? Hit "your": "This is *your* responsibility";

Notice how vocal stress and gesture supplement each other for maximum emphasis.

Now work out the rest of the statements, trying for different shades of meaning and stress.

(2) There is nothing that management can do about this.

(3) I suggest that we work day and night for the improvement of this community.

(4) Pause, if you will, for just a moment; consider the consequences of the course you propose to adopt.

(5) The people of poverty-stricken Asia need your help. What are you ready to do about it?

(6) Let us forget old quarrels. Let us put them behind us and work together from here on.

(7) There are two ways to look at the problem: Obviously better education will be more expensive; equally obviously some limit must be put to public expenditures.

THE LANGUAGE
OF THE SPEAKER

"The right word in the right place"

The average person, faced with the job of making a speech, worries about a lot of things, but probably least of all about the language he should use. Most of us have been brought up in the American school system with the idea that the only language problem is that of writing, and so most of us assume that the problems of spoken language are simply an extension of the problems of written language. This, of course, is far from the truth. To be convinced one need only consider the fact that the speaker may pronounce flawlessly words which he could not spell to save his life; or that the writer may spell words readily without being able to pronounce them. Although this is not the place to start an argument about what constitutes good written style, writing of recognized literary merit is not infrequently completely ineffective for oral delivery. Indeed, if one considers the extemporaneous method as the proper speech method, one should face the fact that rather long-drawn-out compound sentences and the piling up of parenthetic expressions may add up to good oral communication even though they be poor writing.

"The speaker restates his ideas"

Repetition of exact words and reiteration of ideas in different words may read badly, yet when the ear is the only means for taking in ideas, they may not only be acceptable but even advisable. The listener can't go back and reread. It is important, therefore, that he be given the idea again and again if he is to get it. As we have already said, the exact words may be repeated as Lincoln used the word "people" in the classic concluding lines of the Gettysburg Address or the idea may be reiterated in different language to make retention certain. Except in more formal speech, the latter method is undoubtedly better. The salesman may put across to his prospect the virtues of his product through placing it verbally in various functioning situations and stating its superior qualities in each of these situations. By various reiterations he may fix in various minds the idea expressed. The lawyer may set up and fortify an impression by means of analogies, similes, and a variety of descriptive adjectives. The administrator may go beyond one statement of an order — he may give it the quality of a request or an informal recommendation in order to be sure that he gets it across to all his subordinates. After all one man's lethal concoction may be another man's poison.

"The speaker is quotable"

For immediate results and for easy recall on the part of the listener, the speaker will do well to put his ideas into language with a kind of capsule quality. In other words, he will try to be quotable. It is easy to extract slogans or extremely apt remarks from the work of the effective speaker. This use of language might be frowned upon in the more ponderous prose writing, but if the speaker would have immediate results, he will do well to work for this kind of snappy expression. It is all right to talk about putting across the idea regardless of the words but it is still advisable to put the idea in enough different verbal sets to give everyone something tangible to remember. Semantics, the study of the meaning of words, has come to the fore in recent years among specialists in language. The semanticists have made a great deal of the need for speakers and writers to get the word for the thing closer to the thing itself. They have been concerned about the tendency of most people not to distinguish between the fact and the language. To call a man an intellectual will not affect his ability to accomplish involved scholarly things. Many of us, however, are inclined to assume that this scholarly ability goes along with the label "intellectual." The practical speaker will accept this tendency in mankind and provide for it through a bombardment of phrases some of which are bound to get the idea across to each listener in a memorable way.

"Stress is possible in speech only"

There are more than the foregoing basic differences between written and spoken language. Just as spoken language presents the problem of pronunciation instead of spelling so it presents the problem of the proper pause and stress instead of punctuation. The punctuation of written language has been far from satisfactory to those who write most, and it is, as a matter of fact, undergoing far-reaching changes at present. Nor is this hard to understand if one looks at the scant eight or ten specks and hooks and bars to which written language is confined. The advantage that the speaker has over the writer in this connection is tremendous, if not decisive. Take a sentence such as, "Is that so?" and vary its significance first by simply stressing each of the words in order in three separate utterances of the sentence. Go on to add almost endlessly to the shades of meaning by intonation and changes in pitch and rate. It is immediately evident that the spoken word is a much more facile instrument for conveying thoughts and feelings than is the written word.

"Pronunciation: a wilderness and how to get through it"

As far as pronunciation is concerned, we have already called it the spelling of speech. As a matter of fact, although some of my readers will not believe it, it presents even greater difficulties than spelling. Foremost of these is the absence of any final source of authority in pronunciation. In many languages, it is possible to determine not only the length or shortness of vowels, but also the accentuation of syllables through position; in these languages there is very little difficulty in achieving correctness. In English, however, be it British or American, there is comparatively little system or reason. As a matter of fact, English pronunciation is probably the only field in which a large enough number of wrongs makes a right. The traditional 1,000 sheep may approach the cliff, and 999 may leap over to their doom; this does not make it advisable or proper for the one-thousandth sheep to do likewise. If, however, 999 should have chosen to say "a'dult" or "con'tractor," the chances are very good the one-thousandth would do well to surrender and go along with the rest of the crowd even though his dictionary still gives "adult'" and "contract'or." Indeed, if you are of an independent turn of mind, it is quite possible for you to invent your own pronunciations, stick stubbornly to them until you gain a following, and then become a dictator of pronunciation in your own right. Things are not really this bad, of course. The confused speaker who doesn't know whether it's "rătion" or "rātion," "adver'tisement" or "advertīse'ment," will probably be quite safe in going to the dictionary. He should remember, of course, that the most progressive of word books is bound to lag a little behind current popular usage.

That brings us to another source of help for the pronouncer — local usage. The Britisher in using the word "schedule" might as well go ahead and say "shedule." It would be foolhardy for the American to do so. If you are speaking in a neighborhood which thinks of a small stream of water as a "crick," you will gain nothing but suspicion by referring to it as a "creek." Lastly, if you are in "neether-eether" country, you will only succeed in making audiences nervous by saying "eyether" and "neyether," and vice versa. A good suggestion for the speaker who cannot afford to seem either ignorant or affected is to follow the pronunciation practices of some person whose competence and speech background can hardly be challenged. Pronouncing dictionaries are available which will at least provide the alternatives when you are in doubt. I suggest Merriam-Webster's *Guide to Pronunciation* or Kenyon and Knott's *Pronouncing Dictionary of American English* for this purpose.

"Speakers need synonyms"

The extemporaneous speaker must have a vocabulary sufficient for the needs of repetition with variety. If he is an ordinary individual, he will find that he does not have this vocabulary unless he deliberately sets out to build it up. The vocabulary of the average person, even the experienced speaker, is somewhat funnel-shaped. His reading vocabulary — that is, the words he will take a chance on in the process of reading — is comparatively large. This is so because of the practice among readers of making detours around doubtful words in the hope that before the sentence ends the meaning will be made clear. Although this technique does result in occasional embarrassment, all of us use it and it is really very effective. At the writing level, the funnel begins to narrow. Although the average person's vocabulary numbers some thousands of words, he will take chances on far fewer words in his writing than in his reading. He still retains one advantage in his writing in that he may erase or rewrite. When he consults a dictionary and finds his mistake, he can remove it, and as far as his future readers are concerned it will never have been made.

No such luck for the speaker. He is at the narrow end of the language funnel. The number of words readily available to him is strictly limited. He cannot make detours and hope for the best; he cannot erase or speak a cleaner copy; once he has uttered the word, he is stuck with it. What is more, it is stuck in the minds of his listeners. Hence, the courtroom situation in which the attorney extracts a damaging answer to a technically irrelevant question. The opposition asks that it be stricken from the record and the judge so orders. The trouble is that while it is possible to strike words from the record it is impossible to remove them from the memory of the hearer. The extemporizer finds his available supply of words badly restricted by this factor. He would not think of using words in an extempore speech which he might claim for his own in reading or writing. Frequently, too, a psychological factor enters in at this point. The special pressure of the speech situation, with its need for speed as well as accuracy, induces the phenomenon of a word on the "tip of the tongue." You have all heard the speaker who says, "I had that word on the tip of my tongue but I couldn't get it out." The speaker's available supply of language must be well beyond the tip of the tongue. Perhaps the best method for increasing the extemporaneous vocabulary is that of making out lists of synonyms for certain common words. You might start with your present immediately available supply of words which could be used instead of the words "big," "little," "good," and "bad." After you have alarmed yourself sufficiently in this manner, you may go about the business of acquiring new ways of expressing the ideas contained in these words. You are making progress when it is no longer necessary for you to refer to a "good pie," a "good man," and a "good joke" all in the same terms. Since each vocation has its own special ideas and concepts, it is advisable for each speaker to add to his ways of conveying his own most frequently used thoughts. The careful speaker will add slowly to his vocabulary in another direction; he will take note of situations in which he was at a loss for words and will arm himself against a repetition of such a situation. In other words, he will not allow himself to be caught short twice with the same word lack. There are several good books that will help you find synonyms. Roget's *Thesaurus* is an old favorite.

"The speaker uses vivid language"

Language does more than merely label things; it gives ideas meaning, stimulates feeling, and induces moods. It isn't hard to show that the bare naming of thoughts and things is not enough. If we say that a person is very nervous that gives some suggestion as to the condition and its severity. If we say that he is as nervous as a bridge player making a finesse for slam that makes it much more vivid for those of us who play contract. My favorite is still the old expression, "as nervous as a long-tailed cat in a room full of rocking chairs." Whether you want the drab "very," the rather grim "finesse," or the pleasantly vivid "long-tailed cat" will, of course, depend somewhat upon the occasion and the make-up of the group. Certainly the latter two will do much more for the average listener.

Take a few descriptive words and see what you can do to them. Some of the vivid figures are so well known and widely used that they have entered into our language. They are probably a bit worn for our purposes, and should be used sparingly. Work out new ones for yourself or find fresher phrases elsewhere.

Here are some of the old favorites. Have you any newer and better expressions?

hungry as a wolf	wild as a deer
sore as a boil	fat as a pig
cross as a bear	clumsy as an ox
sly as a fox	shy as a violet
as little chance as a snowball in hell	tight as a drum
	thin as a rail
ate like a bird	light as a feather

Try your hand at some of these. What about "as hungry as a late boarder," "as little chance as a Republican in Mississippi," or "as thin as a teen-ager's alibi"?

"Three pitfalls for the smooth speaker"

The speaker should never forget that the style he employs provides one of the very first clues to his personality and leaves one of the strongest impressions upon his listener. If your ideas come out as halting fragments and are expressed in weak and vague words, the listener may not be blamed for reading into your character such qualities as hesitancy, lack of strength, or even general ignorance. If these language weaknesses appear along with the defects of voice and bodily action considered elsewhere in this book the audience has no choice but to assume the speaker's inadequacy. Only when your vocabulary has become a carefully selected tool for the expression of ideas can you hope to move along with the smooth assurance that suggests confidence and authority.

But the speaker who is never at a loss for words may still be ineffective. He may fall into one of the traps which often claim the glib speaker. Chief of these are triteness, pulchritudinous ponderosity, and whatchamacallit language. The habit of using stale expressions frequently fastens itself upon the unfortunate extemporizer. After many painful efforts to make his own language supply fit the needs of the situation, he suddenly discovers that English abounds in ready-made phrases, some of them fine sounding, which he may simply appropriate and use in place of his own. Not only that, but there seems to be at least one of these clichés for every conventional thought the unenterprising speaker may wish to utter. The trouble, of course, is that trite language conveys nothing. It is not communication. The speaker is not speaking — he is reciting, and hence he can expect no response other than a kind of abstract, dilute literary appreciation.

The problem of high-flown, pompous style is again one of misunderstanding. The speaker who concentrates on magnificently rolling phrases and ponderous wording has simply forgotten the purpose of speech. It is possible, of course, that there is a pompous type of person for whom such speaking is inevitable. We are concerned here, however, with the ordinary mortal who, although otherwise normal, has somehow picked up the notion that the note of grandeur constitutes good communication.

The best advice to follow is to avoid unnecessarily long and ponderous words when short words are available. This may, of course, be carried to ridiculous extremes, too, but other things being equal the shorter and simpler the language the better. It is sometimes suggested that the Latin words be avoided except in the most formal expression. This seems extreme advice since occasionally there is no substitute for the long, formal word in securing the effect of legitimate dignity. It is enough here to call attention to the soundness of saying "car," "jaloppy," or even "hot rod" rather than "automotive vehicle" in most circles.

The third habit to be avoided is that of the use of hopelessly vague terminology. Usually this tendency is expressed through certain coined words or phrases. Surely you have been irritated and confused by someone explaining carefully to you how the "whatchamacallit" is fitted on to the "little business," stretched across the "doodad," and extended to the "gizmo" on the "thingamabob." The vagueness of adjectives is perhaps an even more frequent weakness of speakers. As suggested earlier, the speaker who wants to become really effective should set about acquiring just the right adjective for each possible shade of meaning. The overworked old standbys are rarely of much use. After all, it is just as correct to refer to a big flea as to a big whale.

"How rough can you be?"

Now to the question of profanity and colloquial language. What about the speaker and the four-letter words? You know the words I mean. The author finds himself leaning away from the salty but vulgar expressions for more formal occasions but reluctant to go on record as a total abstainer. After all a man who has just hit his thumb with a hammer should be allowed to go well beyond "Good gracious" in the release of his pain. Indeed I have a well-defined feeling that he *ought* to! I remember a colleague of some years ago who seemed to most of the staff a youth of almost unbearable refinement. Some of us were inclined to give him the benefit of the doubt, however. We felt that we should withhold judgment. Then one night we sat near him at the final game of a regional basketball tournament. Our team was one point behind, there were twenty seconds to go when our star guard came out of a mixup under the basket with the ball. The crowd went wild. People screamed and roared as our boys came down the floor with the ball. Our colleague arose in his place and was heard to say, "Defeat them, boys! Oh, defeat them!" That did it. The spirit was there; the meaning was clear enough; the medium was inadequate. The fact that our center missed a lay-up as the gun sounded had nothing to do with our reaction.

Frankly there seem to be occasions that demand violent expression, and in such situations strong language should be used. Naturally if you are a rough diamond and have been invited to address or confer with a group that is known to you to be fussy about strong language you will use restraint. If you are hopelessly addicted to profanity you'd better send someone in your place. The audience is the most important element after all. I once found myself serving on a state committee assigned the task of finding sources for financing a teacher retirement program. With a sour sense of humor or remarkable lack of insight the governor had appointed a practical politician as chairman of this array of educators. He opened the first meeting with the comment, "Frankly, ladies and gentlemen, we got a hell of a job on our hands." Whereas some of us thought these words very neatly described the situation, others present were outraged by the language and resolved not to cooperate with the barbarian who uttered them. Gauge your group as accurately as possible and be guided by what you find. Sometimes the choice of words must involve a calculated risk, but when you know your listeners' tastes use discretion.

A final comment on profanity: Overused it loses all of its value, and I suspect that most of speaking America errs on the side of excess. I think of poor Armenak, a young Syrian whom I once tutored. Before he reached me he had spent several weeks with an uncle in New York. He knew very little English but what he had picked up pretty well makes my point. Armenak always answered in the affirmative with "Damn it yes," and in the negative with "Hell no." He thought that was standard language in America.

What about slang? Should the man who wishes to be an effective speaker avoid all these popular current expressions? The best advice again is not to give up all use of the catchy, sometimes extremely apt phrases of slang. On the other hand they should be used very sparingly. In some circles in high school and college it is almost impossible to understand or be understood in conversation without a thorough grasp of the current expressions. In the rarefied stratosphere of frosty scholarship, of course, slang is unthinkable.

Advantages of popular language are mainly those of freshness and vivid imagery. "Swing" and "rock and roll" are vividly descriptive both in the auditory and visual sense. Being "sent" by music is somehow valid. "Real gone" pretty well covers a number of recognized conditions. On the other hand much slang is neither fresh nor vivid. With over a half million words in the latest Webster it is scarcely necessary to use fly-by-night language to get things said well.

The speaker should be warned about the chief weakness of slang — the fact that it is so short-lived. Very rarely does such an expression remain current for more than a year. Yesterday's "get on the ball" is today's "get with it." One need only attempt to select examples for a text such as this to realize that the slang phrase is the May fly of language. If you employ such expressions do it simply for flavor, not for thought.

"Mr. Smith or Friend Bill"

When should you use first names? What is the persuasive effect of calling Mr. Smith "Bill" the first time you talk to him? Some writers on the subject of human relations have made quite a fetish of this practice. The idea is that a man is pleased and brought closer to the speaker who calls him by his first name. I can only suggest this: Know your listeners — it's possible that as many people are irritated and put on the defensive by this breezy informality as are taken in by it. It is evident that you as an individual must work out the right answer to this problem in each new situation. Certainly it is unwise to assume that everyone to whom you speak will be pleased to be on a "Friend Bill" basis at the first meeting. Perhaps a story will make the point.

Out in Kansas City one afternoon I had the privilege of listening to a debate. Members of one team were well sold on the personal touch. A speaker was down front "Bill-ing and Tom-ing" for all he was worth. After working his way within arm's length of the judge he was demoralized to hear that gentleman say in acid tones, "Young man, will you go back to the rostrum and finish your argument from there!" The budding high pressure operator retreated in confusion. At the end of the debate several of us asked the judge why he had been so hard on the speaker. He answered, "I had to do something. I was afraid that in another minute he was going to throw a cloth over me and give me a haircut and a shave."

What to do, then? Go slow. Study your listener. Don't forget that some people are just as disturbed at being Bill to perfect strangers as they would be at being Mr. Smith to their closest friends.

"Correction is the lesser evil"

Before leaving the matter of language, let's consider the question of what to do once you have made a mistake. There are two lines of procedure open to the speaker who discovers that he has made a mistake in usage or pronunciation: (1) he may ignore the error and go on as if there had been no mistake made; (2) he may correct himself immediately. The first of these has an evident weakness. It is almost certain that some of the listeners will have noticed the mistake and they will probably attribute your failure to correct to ignorance or deceit. The second method is, of course, the only one left for the honest and alert speaker. It is not as good a procedure, of course, as not to have made a mistake at all; nor is it without certain disrupting effect upon the attention of the audience. After all, the pause for correction will break the continuity of expression and temporarily distract attention. It is simply the lesser of two evils. Speakers may take with a grain of salt the dutiful exclamation of close friends among their listeners, "Why, I didn't notice the mistake at all!" Everyone makes mistakes; the point is not to let them upset you. Correct and go on.

"The four methods of presentation"

Everyone who speaks has been faced with the problem of selecting the best method of presentation. Maybe it will be a matter of deciding which method seems best adapted to the individual speaker in a general way; maybe it will involve the problem of picking the best method of presentation in a particular speech situation. One thing is certain; the final decision reached will have a great deal to do with the results obtained. Four methods are usually identified: read, memorized, impromptu, and extemporaneous.

"Reading from manuscript is never very good"

The first of these methods, that of reading a speech from manuscript, can scarcely be recommended despite the fact that one sees it in use on many important occasions. As a matter of fact, the reading of a speech has been a major factor in preventing many a potentially important occasion from becoming notable. In a *Speakers' Manual* issued by the Political Action Committee of the C.I.O. several years ago, the manuscript reading method was dismissed brusquely with the words " — that is no good at any time."

Although this judgment may be a little harsh, there is really very little to be said for reading a speech. The method tremendously reduces or completely eliminates eye contact, it encourages drab and lifeless vocal qualities, and it stifles the true conversational expression. There is a very real question whether reading is a method of speaking at all. It has been perhaps the chief escape of the timid and inept public figure in our day, and the price men of prominence have paid for its use on the platform and over the air must have been tremendous. Certain excuses are frequently advanced for clinging to the method. Speakers whose every remark is a matter of public concern plead that they don't dare not have verbatim manuscripts ready in advance. Although this is a strange confession of incompetence, it provides an alibi with which few have quarreled. Whether we should put much confidence in people who cannot be depended upon to know what they are talking about is another matter.

In presenting material on radio and television programs, it is sometimes argued that the station has a right and ought to have an opportunity to check the speaker's remarks in advance as a reasonable precaution. Although there may be occasions when such precautions are advisable, there is no doubt a tremendous amount of completely uncalled-for manuscript reading on the air. A special hazard in this method lies in the temptation of people to confront the public with little or no advance thought on either the subject or the occasion. This results in a presentation which strongly suggests that the reader is seeing the words for the first time.

The preponderance of read speeches at gatherings of scholars and scientists is usually explained rather lamely on the ground that adequate evidences of cerebration cannot be presented in extemporaneous form. This excuse fails to take into account the natural limitations put upon the amount of heavy and detailed material which can be taken in through the ear. Avoid the reading of manuscripts whenever it is legally permissible in speech situations. Finally, since much of your speaking will be in conference and reading is impractical in the face-to-face conversational situation, you had better practice the extempore method.

"Ghosts and alter egos"

While we are on the subject of the read manuscript what about the reading of ghost-written speeches? It is such a common practice for leaders in nearly all fields to have their talks written for them that there is little use discussing speechmaking unless one takes this matter into consideration. There is a current yarn about the visitor in Washington, guest of a twentieth-century logographer, whose host was approached by a distinguished Senator who had just finished a speech on the floor. The lawmaker said, "That was a fine speech you fixed up for me. It went very well. I hope I have time to sit down and read it this weekend. It seemed to me there's some good stuff in there." This tale not only calls attention to the wide acceptance of ghost writing, but may very well illuminate its most serious threat to thoughtful public address. We may be approaching a period when the dignitary on the platform is merely supplying the voice, the presence, and the excuse for a speech, while all the significant thought and all the effective language are supplied by some unknown at a distant desk.

Not only do Senators, administrators, and candidates lean upon script writers, however. Increasingly the salesman is supplied with flipcards, little answers for all occasions, and a load of miscellaneous detail calculated to relieve him of any necessity for thinking about his product at all. The acquaintance this reader has had with sales personnel in the last decade scarcely supports the fantastic conviction held by some concerns that their agents are such incompetent idiots as to need a full line of predigested patter in lieu of any independent thought. I have even heard of late about embarrassed souls who are required to bring record players along to place before the prospects!

It is true, of course, that the speech writer has been with us from the earliest years of rhetoric; it is equally true perhaps that many a busy man's secretary has become his "alter ego" in times past — his literate self, as someone has put it. This in no way excuses the excesses of recent years. At what, pray, should a statesman be busier than the framing and expressing of his own thoughts on state problems? How useful is the salesman likely to be, if he knows so little about his product and about selling it that he can't be trusted to present it on his own?

"Memorization is rarely worth the time it takes"

The word-for-word memorization of a speech has more to be said for it than the reading. After all it does permit eye contact to the platform speaker and it does give him an opportunity to make his gestures less ridiculous than those of a man with his eyes glued to the reading stand. Nevertheless, it takes real skill and a prohibitively long period of practice to speak from memory in a spontaneous and truly communicative manner. Indeed, the best evidence of effective memorized delivery lies in the failure of hearers to perceive that it has been memorized. Rarely can thoughts and feelings be communicated with maximum effect in memorized language. Since the method calls for a large-scale memorization of specific words and phrases, it practically forces a misuse of preparation time. It is not desirable to memorize your speech.

"The impromptu speech is an emergency measure"

By impromptu presentation we mean the delivery of a speech on the spur of the moment with no time for advance preparation. The impromptu method of presentation may be inescapable in a large number of situations. When it can be avoided, there is little to be said for it.

Speakers who have mastered the art of fluent delivery on short notice, may be led into an overdependence upon the method. But a person who habitually depends upon the inspiration of the moment and makes no advance preparation, even when he has the opportunity, is being vain or lazy or both. There are glib speakers who seem to get up repeatedly and talk and talk in the hope that eventually a worth-while idea will come to them. It's better to bring your ideas with you rather than hope to find them after you arrive.

"The extemporaneous method is most useful"

The extemporaneous method is the most desirable. This involves careful preparation of the ideas, thorough analysis of audience, and intelligent consideration of methods but does not call for the advance selection of exact words. It is the most rewarding both to speaker and audience. The speaker who extemporizes is putting the thoughts in his own words and hence they become in a special sense his own thoughts; inevitably, he feels more responsible for them, more genuinely interested in them. What he says will bear the stamp of his personality. Furthermore, once one has learned to rely upon his own vocabulary, his fluency and the inevitable effect of his language are bound to be increased. Any hesitancy which appears early in the use of the method will soon disappear to be replaced by a firm delivery which will give the speaker genuine satisfaction as being his own. A speaker using this method has another advantage: Since he is not bound to a set comment in specifically memorized words he is able to adjust more easily to emergencies. He is, therefore, a more flexible and more adaptable speaker.

The foregoing advantages to the speaker are for all practical purposes advantages to the listener, too. Audiences prefer to be talked to conversationally and spontaneously, and they derive special satisfaction from the feeling that what they hear comes directly and genuinely from the mind of the speaker and has not been packaged and frozen in advance. The impression of sincerity strongly suggests reliability and we have already considered the importance of this. The extemporaneous method is very helpful in the securing of personal acceptance by audiences. Perhaps the chief virtue of the method, however, lies in the fact that it practically eliminates the possibility of pompous and ponderous oratorical delivery.

EXERCISES

1. *Exactness*

(1) Use the words that do the job. Decide exactly what needs saying, and fit your language to the need. Let's begin with a simple request. "Bring the report."

To whom? "Bring me the report."

When? "Bring me the report right away."

What report? "Bring me the production report for December right away."

Who should bring it? "Miss Roe, bring me the production report for December right away."

What about good manners? "Miss Roe, please bring me the production report for December right away."

Notice how the base statement has been clarified, made more exact, assigned, and made polite. It's done with words.

(2) Try elaborating the following:

1. What time is it?
2. He is a good man.
3. A few people answered.

Find or invent more such statements and work with words.

2. *Choice of words*

(1) Words can do much to set the mood and flavor the facts. Try the following experiment:

Take the following facts and put them first into language that leaves a bad impression, then into language that leaves a favorable impression.

A socialist speaker of some reputation, six feet and four inches tall, weighing 250 pounds, with a receding hairline, having a clear and not very deep voice, talked to a crowd of one hundred people in a hall where the temperature was 68 degrees. He advocated socialized medicine and urged that the federal government nationalize steel and a few other basic industries.

Try for words that slant these facts the way you want them slanted. Is the socialist a red, a Commie, or a liberal, a humanitarian? Does his size make him impressive or ungainly?

(2) Find a paragraph in a paper or magazine. Reduce it to the simple facts, getting rid of the suggestive or colored words. Rebuild the passage in your own words, using all the facts, but giving a different flavor to them.

3. *Pronunciation*

(1) How do you pronounce each of the following? What support do you have for your pronunciation? Are other pronunciations acceptable?

envelope	ration	blue
inquiry	mischievous	news
advertisement	adult	exponent
abdomen	stationery	depot
contractor	schedule	garage
athlete	what	column
automobile	accelerator	vehicle

Find a few other words that puzzle you and look them up in a dictionary.

(2) Pronounce the following passages as precisely as you can, even overdoing it a bit. Record your work and play it back. Keep practicing until you have just the right amount of precision without seeming stilted.

This can't possibly be my problem.
What are you doing?
Where did you put the thirtieth sheet?

John and Tom had hit upon a satisfactory strategy.
Things mustn't be allowed to become worse.
His statistics seem to show promise of improvement.
By and large the present government should suffice us.
This year's profits topped last year's by an appreciable amount.

(3) Careless usage and faulty grammar can damage speaking effectiveness. Persistent use of the following will go a long way toward ruining your influence with literate audiences.

had went	it was him
they was	everybody brought their lunch
he done it	to who did you give it?
I seen	he hasn't done nothing
between you and I	where is he at?

It is pretty generally agreed that if your English is bad, you will do well to take work designed to improve it. Failure to see anything wrong with the above expressions should set you thinking along the lines of a special course in English.

4. *Synonyms*

(1) Collect other ways of saying things. *Use* new words once you have them. The old syndicated column urged that if you used the word three times it would be yours. That is the right idea. Look for words with slightly different shades of meaning. Don't aim at bigger words or fancier words necessarily. Rather get *more* words.

First a preliminary check. How many ways do you have of saying or suggesting the idea of the following?

    big   little   good   bad   go   come   say   ask

(2) How impoverished is your word supply? Are you overworking some of the adjectives? Ponder the different significance of "good" in these: A good cookie. A good joke. A good job. A good girl. Hunt down and list the words you overwork.

(3) Do you have any "whatchamacallit" favorites? Make a list of them. Are any of them necessary? Remember not all these expressions are doodads and thingamajigs; they might easily be mere things and businesses.

(4) Do you go for ponderous and pulchritudinous polysyllables? Are you tempted to use a word just for the way it rolls off your tongue? Are you sure it *is* best, or are you using it because it sounds best? Take the following expressions and put them into plainer language:

> transparently erroneous
> irrevocably committed
> extremely benevolent
> outrageously circumscribed
> monumentally inept
> oleaginous verbiage
> colossal presumption

5. *Methods of presentation*

(1) Watch a speaker who is notebound. Observe how the manuscript interferes with eye contact. Note how it hampers gestures, and how it leads to little unconvincing spurts of energetic delivery interspersed with periods of painstaking reading. Get before a mirror and try reading some passage that is fairly familiar to you. Note how the reading damages communicative behavior.

(2) Memorized delivery isn't recommended as a rule, but if you want to try it remember this: The method by which you memorize is of the utmost importance. Memorize by "wholes" and by thought units. Wherever there is a break in your memorization there is a built-in invitation to forget. For purposes of practice learn the following:

"It has long been the custom of diplomats to assume that there is great virtue in expediency. Thus it is that one sees the representatives of great democracies with long traditions of freedom and self-determination, sitting around the conference table bargaining away the national aspirations of colonials. This is done in the name of realism. To know what is right and to be able to do it, say they, are two different things. If we intend to get along with our old friends in the West, the victims of their imperialist activities will just have to wait for a more auspicious moment if they expect help from us. I urge upon you the consideration of this question: Is there any — ought there be any difference between rightness and expediency? Are virtue and justice ever inexpedient?"

Read this over and over for thought; read it aloud. Eventually the memorization will "happen." Or try the device of taking several runs at each sentence, thus: "It has long been the custom of diplomats. . . ." "It has long been the custom of diplomats to assume that there is great virtue in expediency." Keep this up with each idea unit so that there are no breaks, no artificially welded spots in the language to invite trouble later.

(3) The best way to practice impromptu presentation is to read the news pages of your daily paper, then assign each other topics from the current news of the day with two minutes preparation time. Each speaker should then stand and say what he thinks on the topic assigned. Limit these talks to roughly two minutes at first. Remember to decide first on your purpose and then fix in mind the points you intend to treat. Trust in your available word supply to see you through from there on.

(4) For practice in the extempore method take a current topic from the news. Read all you can find about it. Make a list of ideas you have on the subject. Select a few of these ideas, not more than five if possible. Set these points down in a brief outline, not full sentences necessarily, just cue phrases will do. Find supporting materials for each point. Don't write out the ideas. Bring only the outline to the next session, and make your speech extemporaneously. After you have done this several times, you should try getting the outline in mind, so that you won't even need notes when you get up to speak.

Part Two

The Audience: Who's Listening?

ANALYSIS AND MANAGEMENT
OF THE AUDIENCE

"Good speakers have good audiences"

If it is true that the three main elements in the speech situation are the speaker, the idea, and the audience, it certainly cannot be questioned that the third of these is the most often neglected. As a matter of fact, many would-be speakers appear scarcely to be aware of the bearing of the potential listener upon the speech act. Long hours spent by speakers addressing rows of empty seats in auditoriums and classrooms as a preparation for speaking would seem to be one evidence of this. Another is the frequent presentation of material about which the speaker and no one else in the room cares. Perhaps something may be said for talking before empty rooms, but nothing much can be said in defense of the man who persists in developing subjects in which his listeners could not possibly have the slightest interest. The purpose of speaking is to secure a response, either in thought or action; your listeners are the people from whom you are going to get that response. The purpose of speaking is to communicate an idea or feeling; your listeners are the people to whom that idea must be communicated. The ill-considered attempt to secure certain responses from some audiences can be as unrewarding as the alchemist's attempt to get gold from baser metals. It would, therefore, pay the speaker to examine the emotional-motivational potential of any audience.

"Audiences are moved by broad, basic drives"

For the purpose of audience analysis let us identify two overall areas of motivation. The first of these includes the broad and basic drives — in other words, the ways in which a listener may be expected to respond as a human being. We may list these drives as follows: survival, pride, desire for possessions, desire for adventure, love, hate, and sentiment. It is quite evident that these are not completely separable drives but they will be adequate for the man who wishes to persuade listeners as human beings.

Survival needs very little explanation. The speaker may appeal to self-preservation or social preservation. The former may be reached through inducing fear in the individuals — fear that they will not survive as individuals. An interesting contemporary example of an appeal to social preservation may be had in much that has been written and spoken relating to permanent world peace and the atom bomb. In this appeal, the speaker makes no attempt to argue that the death of the individual will be made more horrible or more final; he simply stresses the probable destruction of the race and intensifies the horror of mass death.

Pride may better be called the fortification of the ego. It is a powerful motive that may be appealed to at the undignified level of flattery — the "I know you are a very shrewd businessman, Mr. Smith," approach. It may also be geared to the demands of social environment — the "keeping-up with the Joneses" angle.

People like to own things. Desire for possessions provides a motive which is very strong although it defies psychological analysis. It has been called the acquisitive instinct, and it is expressed at all levels. Through it you may appeal to the man who collects old string, autographs, or chain stores.

The desire for adventure is a motive which may be depended upon to cut across many of these other apparently more solid appeals. It, too, is a rather hard one for the psychologists to handle, but the persuasive speaker shouldn't neglect it. What other motive appeal can be made effective in the face of pride, possessions, sentiment, or survival? Yet apparently men have turned away from all of these to seek adventure. What else can explain the lure of the Himalayan mountains for people in all walks of life? Notice how often the men who risk their lives on the cliffs and peaks five miles high are engineers, English teachers, authors, and others whose presence there can only be explained on the basis of adventurousness.

The treatment of love and hate as levers for securing certain responses need not keep us long. Everyone knows the blindness of both these emotions, the all-absorbing attention which they command when in full sway, and the attendant "moratorium" on logical and factual appeals.

Sentiment is sometimes looked down upon when defined narrowly, but if one includes in it the feeling of affection for all places and things, its usefulness in controlling responses is evident. Patriotism belongs here. It is a tremendous driving force. The feeling one has for the old home town may also be a genuine and strong one. This sentiment for the old home town is very durable. A speaker before the California Society of Iowans or Nebraskans can bring tears to the eyes of West Coast residents who could not be coerced at gun point into coming back to either of those states but who still feel strongly moved by references to the old familiar places.

"Special motives also govern listeners"

So much for the means by which the listener may be made to respond as a human being. The problem of audience analysis would be a simple one indeed if it could stop here. Sometimes, however, the speaker will appeal to these basic drives with what he considers to be shrewdness and dispatch and yet will not get the response he desires. This brings us to the second broad area of motivation — the special motive appeals. Sometimes your hearer will not respond as a human being because he is a professor, a Presbyterian, an Elk, or a Democrat — in other words because of some social, political, vocational, or fraternal identity which he also possesses. Evidently, we must pursue our query about the listener well beyond his humanness and his probable reaction to the basic drives.

Among the special factors governing response let us consider first that of citizenship. It might make a difference in your results as a speaker if you knew from what town, what state or what nation the bulk of your listeners come. For instance, people in small towns do know more about their neighbors than people in large towns. People in various states are affected by certain identifying elements in their environment. Corn does make its impression upon people who live in Iowa. Great Salt Lake and the Mormon background do impinge upon residents of Utah; and the facts of its one-time independence and great size have done something to Texas.

At the national level, it will probably be wise not to accept for purposes of audience analysis the various national stereotypes. The speaker is not likely to extract much value from the assumption that the Germans in his audience are prone to stubbornness and detailed organization; the Irish to belligerence and eerie romanticism; the Scotch to tightness. He will avoid the mistake of supposing all Englishmen to be humorless; all Frenchmen to be volatile with a slight flavor of moral degeneracy; all Chinese to be possessed of phlegmatic dispositions. There remain for the speaker many levers for moving the thoughts and actions of various nationals which are likely to be peculiar to those nationals — special motives which spring from the racial, political, social, and economic environments of the countries in question. It is proper to warn the student of special-motive appeals not to forget that sometimes other special factors may nullify certain of these reasonably predictable national reactions. A difference in vocational or economic status may very effectively do this. Hence the European movie-goer who got his ideas of Americans from the cocktail-party, idle-rich background of the American movies might have a hard time making an impression on the average American family. Equally the American traveling in Egypt might find himself unable to cope with the comparatively well-fed and comfortable Egyptians with whom he would most likely come in contact after he had geared his thinking of Egyptians to the level of subsistence or actual starvation.

There is a new classification of citizenship that has gained some acceptance — the citizen of the world. As this concept gains more and more currency, speakers will doubtless be obliged to become acquainted with the special set of responses which may be expected from people who give their first allegiance to the world.

The second special area of motive appeal is the vocational. This should need very little elaboration for the readers of this book. The lawyer will at times best be reached as a lawyer. The plumber has his own special interests which have to do with little else than plumbing. And the common laborer, too, is likely to have his own special interests according to the industry in which he is working. It is unrealistic in the extreme for the speaker not to distinguish between the lawyers, plumbers, and ditch-diggers in his audience.

Not completely separable from vocational differences is the question of economic status; and this in turn has a strong bearing upon social strata. Even the choice of similes or examples may be affected for the intelligent speaker by his knowledge of the economic-vocational-social background of his listeners. This is not intended to encourage snobbery or to contribute to the setting up of a caste society in America; it is simply to suggest that the areas of experience open to people of varying wealth, vocational interests and social identities are not likely to be the same. As a result the person who would control the responses of people representative of these various groups must talk their language and deal in their interests.

A third factor in determining probable audience response is the educational background. Education not only provides detailed facts and techniques to those who are educated, but also attempts to provide certain attitudes. Differences in education among members of his audience must concern a speaker. These differences will determine what examples it would be well to use with a certain audience. Classical allusions are more likely to have a point for the college-educated listener, for instance; whereas similes based upon assembly-line mechanisms would have more significance for a factory worker. Quotations from Shakespeare, at least in Elizabethan English, are likely to mean more to the man who has studied literature than to the man who has not. Occasionally an audience of people who have not gone to college will be completely up to following your classical and literary allusions. It is simply safer to avoid too strong a reliance upon the content of the college course with non-college audiences.

In connection with this factor, avoid overuse of the jargon of some narrow field of specialization. In addressing groups which are not familiar with his field, many a specialist has failed to convey his knowledge to popular audiences because they didn't know what his words meant. It is advisable not to assume too much in the way of detailed technical knowledge from any general audience. Any enthusiastic specialist is likely to be carried away. Watch yourself.

From the standpoint of cultural background, it is usually safer to assume more of the high school graduate than of the listener who never finished grade school; and more of the college-educated listener than of the high school listener.

The sex of the listeners will be a determining factor in choice of subject, supporting material, and language. It is quite evident that the basic differences in intelligence are more of kind than of degree as between man and woman. Actually, as far as probable ability to comprehend what you had planned to say goes, there is no significant difference. Men have no reason to be patronizing in their selection of ideas for presentation to audiences of women; but there are a few things which the speaker should consider carefully in the matter of sex differences.

The first of these is the environmental factor. Women, by and large, will discuss clothing and hair styles with much more fervor and intentness than men; they will talk about sewing and cooking with more sustained enthusiasm. They have been brought up to do so and they may be depended upon in a large number of cases to follow through. The war plant activities of recent years have indicated that the ability of women is remarkable, not to say alarming, in many of the more purely mechanical activities once thought peculiar to men, but in general they will be more certainly interested in traditionally feminine matters.

Men, on the other hand, are likely to be interested for substantially the same reasons in baseball scores, reciprocating engines, and other "peculiarly male matters." References in these areas of special traditional interests of men and women are much more likely to be effective with audiences made up wholly of either men or women.

In view of frequent manifestations of singularly bad taste on the part of people talking before mixed groups, it is probably a good idea to deliver a warning here. Under no circumstances should the speaker use sex jokes before mixed audiences. It is not a question of prudery; it is simply good sense not to risk embarrassing your audience.

There seems to be some support for the theory that whereas men are better able to grasp the broad concepts women are better able to master the details. Certainly women are much better listeners than men when the material is tedious and elaborately itemized. As a matter of fact women will show more determination in staying with the speaker who goes on for long periods in speeches loaded with the minutiae of the subject. I think it is correct to go a step farther and say that women try harder to listen than men do. I trust that this will not act as an encouragement to boring talkers before feminine audiences. After years of marveling at what women will endure at P.T.A., Women's Club sessions, and the like I feel safe in suggesting that perhaps they find less need for lively style and humor than do men.

How old are the members of your audience? Naturally, it is not always possible to extract much profit from a consideration of this question. Too many audiences run from infant to octogenarian. However, there are times when a speaker can generalize better if he can see that his audience is young or old. Some experts would try to put a middle-age class in here too, but for audience analysis purposes, there is no middle age. The people who usually come in this class may better be thought of as the young-old or the old-young. Nevertheless, there are certain occasions upon which the speaker confronts an audience which is definitely young and possessed of the characteristics of youth, or definitely old. What may we generalize about the reactions of youth?

First, the humor of the young is likely to be broader; the comedy nearer to slapstick. On a campus where I once worked we had a group of talented young men who presented an annual show which caused a considerable uproar because of the nature of the jokes used. The older element have had no trouble with the double meanings — they have at times worried over the more obvious biological references. Here we have a situation that thwarts correction. If the broad humor is curbed to the satisfaction of older critics, the younger element turns away from the show as dull and lacking in entertainment. This pretty well reveals the difference in the tastes of young and old in matters of humor. You as a speaker can make something of this if your audience is homogeneous. Youth, by and large, is more responsive to the appeals of adventure. It is inclined to be radical, or perhaps one should say, it wants to do something about the problems which beset the race; hence, it can be actuated readily. One may safely act upon these observations even though everybody knows at least one hidebound reactionary of eighteen and a comparatively ancient radical idealist or two.

As to the characteristics of the old upon which the speaker may rely, perhaps the foremost is conservatism. Whether from the wisdom of years or sheer weariness of spirit, older people are less subject to violent responses, spontaneous agreements, and whole-hearted denials. Hence, the speaker is likely simply to have set his fifty-year-old listeners to thinking by the time the twenty-year-olds are anxious to be up and doing. Life being a bruising experience at best, a certain skepticism and wariness is usually apparent in those who have lived longer. Perhaps one should add to this a reference to the tendency of the old to incline more to gentle sentiment than to fervor. And finally, for the speaker to tread upon the opinions of older listeners is a much more dangerous thing than to suggest new directions to the young. In this connection I recall how my father, a lifetime Republican, used to arise in his wrath and turn off the television set when a Democratic candidate appeared on the screen. It took a little kidding about fairness and confidence to get him to listen to the opposition at all. As he used to put it, "I'm old enough to know what I know."

"The listener is affected by his situation"

The last of the specific factors we may call the immediate audience environment — the occasion, in other words. It is possible that the fact that you are speaking on the Fourth of July or Mother's Day should be more influential in determining the predictable responses of your listeners than all of these other things. There are ways in which people behave in church, for example. The occasion of a Sunday morning sermon, the churchly atmosphere, can make some people almost unrecognizable. A man may present one audience ensconced behind the desk at his place of business and a far different one with his feet propped on the clubhouse rail. As a general thing, men just don't talk shop at dinner; although even here there may be a distinct difference between the get-acquainted luncheon of busy men and the more purely social dinner-at-home situation. Similarly, subtle differences are noticeable between the situation in which the speaker stands and the listeners are seated, both speaker and listeners are seated, or the speaker is seated and the listeners are standing.

Too little attention is devoted to the technique of speaking while sitting down. Many of our effective public speakers, indeed, have neglected this so completely that they lose much of their effectiveness when speaking while seated.

It was frequently noted that Hitler never talked in small group meetings — he always made speeches. If you can get away from radio and television for conversation at home this will be your best chance to practice "sit-down" speaking. Insist on real conversation — not sloppy "yep" and "nope" exchanges.

"Radio and television listening is different"

Audience response and the control of audience response are considerably complicated on the popular mass media of radio and television. In the radio situation, obviously both speaker and listener are cut off from the benefits of immediate and direct visual contact; they lose the common advantage of gesture, posture, and facial expression. In TV the listener sees the speaker but the speaker is still unable to see the audience. But there are other situational differences. The speaker's immediate environment in the studio is likely to include an audience which he can see and which is seated in a comparatively large group, as well as a battery of microphones and cameras which remind him rather inadequately of another audience seated comfortably in small groups in innumerable kinds of surroundings and over an area of hundreds of miles. It is highly questionable if any man is competent to cater fully to the speech needs of both these audiences at once. Just as you do not deliver speeches before your family in the parlor, so you do not give fireside chats before audiences of 500 people in a large and acoustically unreliable hall. Yet the public speaker whose voice may rise as he sways a large audience at the convention may sound like a half-hysterical ham when his voice comes from your living room television set.

The problem of just how the speaker is eventually going to be effective with this completely unpredictable audience in a completely unpredictable environmental situation has not as yet been solved. Present experience would seem to indicate that higher speed, the use of more sustained and more obvious attention-getters, and unfortunately a less exhaustive treatment of the subject are all helpful in preventing the listeners wherever they are, from turning the knob. About all that can be recommended definitely, however, for the radio and TV speaker is that he become an effective speaker according to the old and time-honored rules of speech. This will be his best protection against failure.

EXERCISES

1. *Audience management*

(1) Find in a presidential report to the nation evidence that the speaker has analyzed his vast audience. Has he done it effectively? See if you can find appeals of the following kinds:

survival	patriotism
pride	hate
desire for adventure	

(2) Prepare about 250 words designed to win support for a new recreation center from:

young people	old people
men	women
property owners	non-property owners

(3) You are trying to sell a five-year-old automobile. It's a two-door hard-top, red with black trim, power brakes, power steering, and window controls. There is a cigarette burn on the back seat. The speedometer reads 55,000 miles.

Your prospect is a teen-ager after his first car.

Your prospect is an elderly man whose wife is along.

What will you say, and what points will you stress in each of the situations?

(4) You are to introduce a Yugoslavian official to a small town forum audience. What will you say? Will you call attention to the Communist identity of his country or ignore it? Will you make any light references to the obvious delicacy of the situation? Will you mention United States' gifts to Yugoslavia?

(5) You are addressing a group of Jewish merchants. Will you tell a story in Yiddish dialect? Will you make remarks based on traditional Jewish qualities? If you have to mention the Israel-Egyptian conflict will you take sides in any way or will you try to be neutral?

(6) Prepare a hundred words explaining the misdeeds of a labor leader or a banker to a meeting of business men, then do the same for a union meeting.

(7) Take a copy of Lincoln's *Gettysburg Address*, extracts from Churchill's *Their Finest Hour*, or a passage from Webster's *Reply to Hayne*. Sit down at a table and read this material with as much force and feeling as you can muster. How did it feel? Did you feel inhibited or restrained by the fact you were seated? Try the same thing with an editorial from a newspaper. Practice this kind of talking until the unnatural feeling wears off.

(8) Get in front of a microphone and use the same materials suggested in Exercise 7. Try to visualize a group of listeners seated easily in a living room or TV room. Notice the special difficulty of getting adjusted to this situation in which you can't see the audience. Try for poise and directness under these circumstances.

ATTENTION

"Audiences often have prevailing moods"

Often a consideration of the motives just discussed will make it possible for the speaker to identify the prevailing attitude or mood of the audience before he addresses it. These prevailing audience attitudes may be listed as follows: (1) agreement and acceptance; (2) indifference or suspended judgment; and (3) hostility or opposition. The first of these is not necessarily as pleasant for all concerned as it might seem. Many a speaker has seethed inwardly in frustration as a smiling audience pleasantly accepted everything he said. The speaker who wants action more than "amen" sometimes feels that his words are being literally smothered in sweet acceptance. The perfectly agreeable audience can be maddening to the speaker who wants results. The writer has been asked by dozens of fund raisers how to get prospective contributors to quit congratulating them on the worth-whileness of their cause and to dig down after the money. He has commiserated with harassed insurance salesmen who encountered the impenetrable wall of absolute verbal agreement and came away without results. If your audience belongs in this category, your best means for moving them is through the emotional appeals. Added logical-factual materials are likely to be futile. Tell them good businessmen and sound citizens have all done what you want them to do; tell them they owe it to their loved ones; tell them the man down the street has already done it; remind them that faith without works is dead — that there is something a little ridiculous about passive agreement. You might have to be a little hard on them — for their own good, of course.

Let us turn to a consideration of the audience that seems to be predominantly without any feeling either way about you or your subject. This audience is waiting to be moved and your first responsibility is to gain their interest. Acquaint them with the problem you wish to solve, make vital to them the information you wish to communicate, and it usually is easier to get results from them than from the first type. We have already discussed the necessity of becoming the spokesman of the listeners. This is especially important with fundamentally indifferent audiences. Make deliberate efforts to interest these people in your ideas by referring to common ground, by giving them good reason to believe that their previous lack of interest was strictly an oversight which can now be corrected, and by relating your idea to their experience and needs.

"Getting a hearing from hostile listeners"

One of the most challenging problems that the speaker may face is that of securing a hearing from a hostile audience. The following methods should apply whether the situation be one in which a well-liked speaker presents an unpalatable idea or a disliked speaker presents an idea which is not particularly objectionable.

The first method to be recommended is the absolute frankness approach. Here a speaker begins by recognizing the hostility toward himself or his idea. He comes right out and says "I know you don't like me" or "I know you won't like what I am going to tell you." Having thus put his cards on the table, he has more or less challenged the sportsmanship of the listeners.

74

Most audiences in most situations will respond and the speaker will have his hearing. If you challenge the average man on his sense of fair play, he will be fair if it kills him.

The second method is the mood of agreement. To achieve this, the speaker starts by making several statements with which few, if any, of the people in his audience can disagree. He asks questions with "yes" answers and soon his listeners realize that they have a lot in common with him. They find it easier to say "yes" to the really key questions. Start with your listeners as human beings — "No man likes to be alone." Go a little closer; touch them as Americans — "Our country is based on its citizens' will to cooperate." Move closer — "This state can be proud that it was one of the early defenders of democracy." Now to the town or area — "This city of ours is a cooperative enterprise. It is great because its people have worked together." Now your listeners are in the spirit — they are saying "yes." Now make your proposal. Thus a mood of agreement may be used to get a hearing from listeners who come determined not to give it.

The third sound procedure may be called the method of concession. Frequently, you may gain personal acceptability and a good hearing for your proposal by starting right out with a few admissions not only of the lack of perfection in your plan or product but of the validity and good qualities of competing plans and products. If the speaker doesn't carry this too far and if he always remembers to follow each concession with that all-important "however," this may be one of the most disarming of the approaches to an ill-disposed listener.

A fourth method — and one recommended here with some hesitation — is that of making your proposal logically inescapable. The speaker presents the facts and arguments so overwhelmingly that the mind must accept them regardless of feelings toward the speaker or his proposal. If you are sure that your listeners are uniformly intelligent and reasonable and if you are sure that they have ample time, you may attempt this method. It is recommended reluctantly because most of us have seen ideas rejected even when all reason and evidence seem to cry for their acceptance. The method is unreliable because people so rarely do what, beyond all reasonable doubt, they should be doing.

"Attention is given through the senses"

A great deal has been said about the necessity for commanding the attention of listeners. It is as true as it was when the psychologist William James said it, that "what holds attention, determines action." Attention from his listeners is absolutely essential, then, to the successful speaker. But just what is attention and how is it manifested? How do listeners attend to speakers? And can we expect 100 per cent attention? As to how people attend, it is quite evident that they do so through the ear and the eye. The auditory sense is the main medium through which the listener follows along with the speaker, but when the speaker is within view of the audience, the visual sense is also important. The auditory and visual evidences of attention go together as a matter of fact, hence a group of people gathered around a radio listening to a speaker are likely to have their glances fixed upon the expanse of cloth and wooden slats in front of the receiving set at time when they are being most attentive very much as they would with television. The "attentive" look provides the best means that the speaker has for checking on the attentiveness of an audience.

Attention being as important as it is, the speaker is occasionally tempted to employ devices for getting attention only to find that he has it where he doesn't particularly want it. For example, the speaker may engage in some wild and eccentric action or may bellow occasionally to stir flagging attention, and then discover that his listeners are attending to his peculiar actions and tones, whereas the idea he is trying to communicate is attended to no better than it was before. Any physical actions or variations in pitch and volume should be related specifically to the idea, should be motivated by that idea and should intensify the listener's attention to the idea. A man with eccentric actions,

The Saturday Evening Post

"AS I WAS SAYING . . ."

distracting voice mannerisms or attention-splitting peculiarities of diction is likely to be his own worst enemy.

As for 100 per cent attention, the wise speaker doesn't expect it. Undivided attention is probably out of the question. What you should aim at is a good percentage. All of us have heard speeches on subjects so inherently interesting that we attended at the start in spite of obstacles set up by the speaker, only to find ourselves losing interest as the speaker continued his deadly work. We have also had the experience of starting "cold" as listeners to intrinsically dull subjects only to be carried away by effective presentation to the point where we attended closely. Sometimes, of course, the basically interesting subject presented by an effective speaker will not hold attention because of some element in the physical environment. Hard and uncomfortable chairs may be a factor here. A thwarting position behind a column or other visual obstruction may cancel out the best attention-getting attempts. The writer has been in speech situations where for sheer improvement of attention one raised window would have been worth five striking illustrations.

"Some good attention-getters"

There are certain devices which are almost unfailingly effective in gaining or reclaiming the attention of listeners. One of these is the *story*. Whether man has an inherent weakness for a good story or whether the taste is cultivated through a childhood of bedtime stories makes no real difference. The point is that the prospect of a story makes everyone sit up and listen, and the speaker who has a good story and tells it well has two strikes on any audience. The story may be used in the very beginning to fix attention, it may be used anywhere in the speech to reestablish flagging attention, or it may render the conclusion memorable. It may be dramatized vividly or it may be delivered without any flourishes. Some storytellers feel that attention is better assured when a wide range of volume and radical changes in rate are employed. It seems to the writer that if the audience is so far gone as to need such measures it may be too late. More violent gestures may contribute to the process of arresting attention when it has been lost. I incline to the idea, however, that the chief virtue of the story lies in the form and language rather than in eccentricities of presentation.

"Questions demand answers"

The *question* is effective for getting attention. Since the earliest days of speechmaking this device has been used with good results. When the listener is asked what he thinks of a certain line of procedure or what his opinion is of someone under discussion he tends immediately to try to frame an adequate answer, and in his effort to do this he attends with special care to what the speaker has to say. Just as long as a question causes this focusing of the audience's forces, speeches will continue to be introduced by questions. There will almost certainly be times when this device will be worth trying in your speaking.

"The tie-in invites attention"

Another good method for concentrating attention upon what you have to say may best be called the *tie-in*. This consists simply of taking a little time to indicate your awareness of what has gone on before you got up to speak. Frequently, when you take the floor or first gain an audience with an interviewee your listener's attention is still focused on what he was doing or hearing before you came in. You can hasten the transfer of his interest to your remarks by making some brief reference to what has gone before. This not only provides a release for the listener but is likely to enhance the speaker's personal prestige. Surely all of us have been irritated by the speaker who comes barging into our consciousness unheralded and without preliminaries and goes blindly and stubbornly ahead with what he came to say as if he operated in a vacuum. Suppose a man has been exposed all day to a succession of desperately serious reports, each submitted in its own little compartment and as if nothing else existed. It is easy to see that a little relaxed comment indicating awareness of the outer world would come to such a man like water in a desert.

"Challenging statements, startling statements and paradoxes also work"

The *challenging statement* with its suggestion of doubt as to the listeners' ability to do what they are being called upon to do, also draws attention. As soon as a man casts doubt on our motives or capacities, we become alert and attentive. After all, if we are not carefully on the defensive, how shall we show him

79

up? The challenge with a flavor of antagonism must be used sparingly, as when the speaker begins by saying, "I suppose I'm wasting my time telling you this," or, "Of course you can't do much about this problem." This must be done with due reference to the comment contained in *The Virginian*, "When you say that, smile."

Sometimes the public speaker may find suspense the best means of sustaining attention. A generation brought up on the soap opera will always be around for the next episode. I heard a very fine example of suspense built up by withholding the solution while developing several extremely knotty problems for the audience. The speaker introduced a whole series of questions as follows: What if the French won't fight? Can we trust West Germany? Are the Japanese just waiting for a chance? Is Italy worth having on our side?, and so on. Finally, when the audience was literally swamped in problems, each intensified to the ultimate degree, the speaker came through with some encouraging answers.

In the narrative speech the possibilities are almost unlimited. The storyteller can build suspense almost at will by keeping his listeners guessing as to the outcome of his tale.

In speaking for immediate results in most fields, however, long sustained suspense is rarely feasible. If obscurity is going to interfere with your purpose even for a short while, suspense will lose more than it will gain.

The *startling remark* is also a good attention-getter. A lecturer on cancer recently jarred his audience by holding up a cigarette and saying, "Twelve hundred men committed suicide last year with guns. During that period ten million people used the cigarette for the same purpose."

At an education convention last year a speaker began a speech with the statement, "You're a chump to stay in teaching." We all listened carefully. I have often made a bid for the attention of a fading class by asking the question, "What time is it?" Students, shocked to find the instructor thinking along the same lines as they have been, are perceptibly more alert for a while.

The *paradox*, or self-contradictory statement, may be very useful in laying hold upon audience attention especially at the beginning of a speech. Recently, a speaker at a meeting of oil men opened his remarks with the statement, "If we keep on building America at the present rate, there will soon be nothing left of it." This is a typical paradox. In its effective combination of suspense and challenge, the paradox has no equal as an introductory device. Avoid the too evident reaching for paradox or the use of ill-devised paradoxes in which the contrast is not vivid.

To summarize the problem of attention, don't expect perfect attention, remember that your only levers are visual and auditory, pay attention to your audience if you want their attention, select facts and examples with impact, get clear and vivid language, use variety of pitch and speed, and try silence occasionally to bring your audience back.

EXERCISES

1. *Prevailing moods*

You are trying to meet a quota for the blood bank. Prepare a fifty-word appeal calculated to get action from an indifferent group. Do the same for a group that is given to lip service, and for a group that is openly disapproving of the whole idea of blood-giving.

2. *Attention-getters*

Work out attention-getters for the following situations:

(1) You have taken the floor right after a very amusing speaker. The crowd is still chuckling. Your topic is serious and important.

(2) You are trying to sell life insurance to a man who is known to have expressed an unfavorable opinion of insurance in all its forms.

(3) You have been talking for about forty minutes and have about ten more minutes of significant material to present. Your listeners are getting openly restless and inattentive.

Check the next speech you hear for "tie-ins," rhetorical questions, shock statements, and stories. Did the speaker use any of them? All of them? Did they seem effective in helping him to hold attention? Did you notice any places where any of them might have been used to advantage?

3. Helping yourself to attention

(1) You have called a meeting in your office. There are five people present. You have three comfortable chairs, two small and squeaky chairs. Two of the group are facing an afternoon sun at your window. The temperature is about 65. You didn't organize your talk — figured you needn't bother with that in an informal session. You called the meeting for five-thirty on Friday evening and it will take about an hour. What can you do to improve the attention at this meeting?

(2) Next time you find it hard to listen to a speaker, analyze the situation. Jot down a list of the things that kept you from listening.

Part Three

The Idea: What's Being Talked About?

SUBJECT AND PURPOSE

"The subject is usually provided"

In formal courses in speaking, a great deal of attention is frequently given to the selection of a subject. As a matter of fact, this is not a very serious problem in a large number of speech situations and is not likely to concern the prospective speaker at all on most of the speech occasions. Once you get out of the artificial classroom situation, your subjects are usually ready-made. A man takes the floor because something that has been discussed or proposed in the mass meeting, council session, or directors' meeting has made it advisable for him to give his ideas and feelings on the subject. Even in the more formal speech situations a topic is usually assigned. You will have many more invitations to talk on some specific subject than you will just to come and talk. Often the nature of your job and the basis of your reputation dictate what you will talk about. The problem here, then, is predominantly not one of what subject to use but of how best to develop and present the subject already provided.

Of course, if one becomes a professional lecturer and goes about talking to audiences who must pay to hear him, the selection of a subject becomes more important. For such a speaker, the stress must be carried even beyond the selection of a subject; the wording of the title itself must be made catchy. For most of us, however, it is safe to say that concern for a title to our remarks is extremely small. The insurance salesman doesn't announce to his prospect that he is now going to talk for five minutes on something snappy such as "How to Live Happily Ever After," or "A Matter of Life or Death." The lawyer does not ask the judge to introduce him to the jury and announce his subject as "It Might Have Been You" or "Society Is the Real Criminal." Nine times out of ten the personnel man goes about his business of influencing morale without announcing he is about to discuss some such subject as "You Don't Have to Work Here" or "It's Your Business."

"How to pick a topic"

If you have been asked to make a speech, and the assignment is not more definite than that, then the question arises of what to talk about. Consider the following sources. Your best leads will lie here. First, review the various fields of special interest about which you know most. After all it's *you* they have asked to speak. Don't be afraid to talk shop. Examine the possibilities of your own field of activity. Your own vocational interests might well be made the topic of a fine speech.

What about your hobbies? Often a man feels that his sideline activities can't possibly be of any interest to others — as often as not he is wrong to feel this way. The very appeals that drew you to a hobby will very likely work upon your audience in the same way.

There is a well-established agreement among writers and speakers that the two most interesting sources for topics are the very well known and the completely new and strange. For a good companion on train or plane there is no one like the man who has been to strange and exotic places — unless it be the man who turns out to have come from the old home town. If you can't regale them with tales from the South Sea Islands, tell them about the old corner drugstore and what happend to the gang that used to hang out there.

In terms of audience appeal these two sources are about even. Deal in the commonplaces — the things that will strike a familiar note with your listeners. People want to hear about the people they know. They smile at the troubles of the kid next door, they worry about the problems of the folks down the street. Audiences like to feel that they are on familiar ground. If such ideas are made vivid by lively presentation they will please people.

As for the exotic, the strange and different, not very many of us have the background for such topics. If you have been places and seen things — *and have reacted to your experiences* — you are ready for most audiences. I recall a friend of mine who was the envy of us all. He held an able seaman card and had traveled all about the earth, visiting all the lands we dream about. The trouble was, as we found out upon his return, he hadn't reacted to any of this experience except in the most routine and prosaic ways. Yes, he had been through the Panama Canal, but all he brought back from it was a kind of tourist post card, "kiss of the oceans" approach. True, he had spent weeks in Egypt, but about all he brought away was the "camel against the sunset," Baedeker Sphinx routines. And a final warning: Most of us would as soon listen to a report on someone's operation, well told, as to watch those colored slides you took last year in Arizona, if you can't give us that little extra detail that makes them special.

Check the occasion on which you are to speak. The occasion often suggests good subjects. The patriotic holiday session might call forth a eulogy of some great national leader or an appreciation of national strength or virtue. It might even provoke a warning or a plea for re-examination of our world position on key issues. It's true that some people can manage to work any situation around until it provides an excuse for their favorite remarks. There was the office in which the personnel used to wonder each day what the boss would talk about besides his new grandson. Sometimes a justifiable use may be made of occasions to bring attention to rather remote matters that nonetheless need talking about. In a speech at the dedication of a federal building Theodore Roosevelt took the opportunity to deliver some famous remarks on "Muck Raking." A fine prophetic vision of a future great America was given by Daniel Webster at the dedication of the Bunker Hill Monument. And in more recent times Winston Churchill has used a commencement service at a small Midwestern college as the occasion for a key utterance on international policy. More often, however, the occasion will suggest topics that relate definitely to it. To put it another way, a Fourth of July picnic may safely be eliminated as the place for your talk on how to make delicious devil's food cake or your pet treatise on how to tie trout flies.

Once in a while it is wise to talk "from ignorance." That is to say if you are talking at a dinner of transportation men, and you know very little about the hauling business, you can give them a very interesting time by providing them with the *lay* reaction to various problems involved in transportation. I have used this approach with success before a number of professional clubs and conventions.

"The purpose is all-important"

Generally the practical speaker in a practical situation doesn't have to worry about a subject. The subject is at hand. His real concern has to do with *purpose*. In other words, in discussing the subject he must decide just what purpose he intends to achieve. This matter of purpose cannot be stressed too much for speakers. It should be perfectly plain that no effective purpose is accomplished by people who have not set out to achieve definite goals. Be sure to get your objective clearly in mind before you start talking. If your speech is to be impromptu — that is, if you are going to speak out in a meeting because you can't keep still any longer — take time to think out in a specific sentence just what your purpose is going to be. Even on such short notice you must take time for this. You always have time to figure out your purpose. Anything you are likely to say without a specific purpose will be better unsaid anyway. Ordinarily, of course, when you have a little more time, a few minutes or a few hours, the first step in speech composition should be to write out in a full sentence the purpose of your speech. If your speech is primarily persuasive, this may be expressed in the form of a statement of the response desired. The desired response listed for each assignment in Part Four is a matter of general purpose. The specific purpose must be worked out for each speech as it comes along. For example, if your general purpose is to inform your listeners, your specific purpose might be to tell the listeners how to select a suburban house, how a bill becomes a law, or how to get on a quiz program.

EXERCISES

How to pick a topic

Analyze your personal supply of possible topics for speech. Make a list for each of the following areas of interest:

1. Early life experiences
2. Places where you have lived or visited
3. Jobs you have held
4. Interesting non-vocational assignments you have had
5. Your hobbies or sidelines
6. Your associations with well-known people
7. Associations with less well-known but interesting people

Analyze at least three speeches you have heard recently. Answer the following questions about each of them:

1. Did the speaker draw primarily on personal experience and knowledge?
2. Did he bring a new and fresh viewpoint to fairly common materials?
3. Did he make use of unusual experiences in the speech?
4. Was the topic one that only this speaker could have discussed?
5. Did most of the ideas seem to come "second hand"?

The Specific Purpose

You have been asked to speak about your work on the community chest drive. What purpose will you try to accomplish? Will you:

1. Simply make an appeal for further support of the drive?
2. Urge upon the audience the addition of certain activities not now included?
3. Suggest specific increases in pledges for your listeners?
4. Recommend an overall change in the drive?
5. Appeal directly to this audience for help in carrying on the campaign?
6. Simply report on the progress of the drive to date?

You have been asked to introduce the guest speaker at an important dinner. Will you:

1. Stress his accomplishments in the field to be discussed?
2. Tell some little-known facts about him?
3. Let the listeners know what makes this man an especially good speaker for the occasion?
4. Stress your guest's reputation as a speaker?
5. Simply tell jokes at his expense?

Analyze three speeches you have heard recently. Check the following for each of them:

1. Was there a clear-cut specific purpose?
2. Was it stated early and unmistakably?
3. Were you obliged to guess at the purpose?
4. Was there no discernible purpose?
5. Did the speaker always remember his stated purpose?
6. Considering everything, were you disappointed in the purpose selected by this speaker in this situation?

7

SELECTION AND ARRANGEMENT
OF POINTS

"Use few points"

Having decided upon your specific purpose and having either chosen or been confronted by your subject, you will take the next step — that of selection and arrangement of main points. Although, of course, this may not be made a hard and fast rule, it is advisable not to go beyond five in the number of main points. This is simply a question of efficiency. It is doubtful that the listener will make much of ten or fifteen points presented in rapid succession. He is much more likely to remember all of three points than he is to remember any of eight or nine. The element of available time enters here, too. If the speaker has a half-hour in which to develop a subject and there are seven phases of the subject which occur to him, on each of which he feels he ought to spend ten minutes, his problem is one of selection. He might decide to develop three of these points for approximately ten minutes apiece; he might decide to treat three of them at some length and throw in the other four as best he can; he might decide to touch lightly on each of the seven or he might decide to go as far as he can and stop when the time is up.

Ordinarily, it is better to do the first of these things — give an adequate treatment of a smaller number of selected points. Having arrived at a list of all the points which could be considered, the speaker may limit and select intelligently along the following lines. He may choose those points which are most likely to appeal to his particular audience. He may consider the points on which he is best informed or in which he is most interested. Possibly he may get a clue from the occasion or perhaps he *must* use certain of these points if he is to accomplish his purpose.

We have been talking here, of course, about limitation and selection of points where time demands it. Actually, the foregoing recommendations apply in practically all speech situations even when theoretically the speaker has all day. There is a very definite limit to the amount of elaboration which the average listener can assimilate whether he has an hour or ten minutes; and it is a good general rule for the speaker to keep down the number of points. But having selected the points, you have the job of arranging them in the best order or at least in a good order.

"There are several methods of arrangement"

Several methods of arrangement are worth considering; such as inductive, deductive, causal, chronological (either narrative or process), problem-solution, and "string of beads" or accidental. Here again it is quite likely that a lot of fussing is unnecessary. Frequently your subject and purpose will force upon you a certain kind of arrangement. If your purpose is to state a problem and suggest a solution, your form of arrangement is all settled for you. If you are explaining an experiment, step by step, or telling about a vacation trip, a time order is inescapable. If it is your purpose to identify a cause, logical order of cause and effect is a must. The following examples are worth looking over.

PROBLEM–SOLUTION PATTERN

Let's Face It: The Guaranteed Annual Wage

I. There is a need in the United States for the guaranteed annual wage, because
  A. Unemployment is still a major problem
    1. In seasonal industries
    2. Among workers in marginal industries
    3. During retooling and plant development periods and because
  B. Present means for insuring laid-off workers' income are inadequate, since
    1. Most states' unemployment insurance laws provide only a small amount,
      a. Some states give as little as $20 weekly
      b. None give more than ½ of normal pay, and
    2. In an era of credit and payment plans this is bad economy, for
      a. It causes hardship for workers
      b. It also does damage to retail trade, and because
  C. The payroll of labor is the most important element in our national income, since
    1. Wages add up to over 80 per cent of our buying power
    2. The lower income brackets supply most of our income tax.
II. The guaranteed annual wage is practicable, since
  A. It puts an industrial cost on the industry where it belongs, since
    1. Company A provides funds for its own workers only
    2. Out of its own income, and
    3. Doesn't have to support other ill-stabilized industries' working staff, and because
  B. This cost is not burdensome, since
    1. Over 200 such plans are already functioning, for example:
      a. Nunn-Bush
      b. Hormel Packing.

2. The automobile industry is experiencing no trouble with recent plans, for
    a. Recent lay-offs in Detroit were cushioned for workers
    b. Proposals are not for cutting down of auto industry plans, but for extending them.
III. Therefore we may assume that the industries of the United States should adopt the guaranteed annual wage, because
    A. The need is great for guaranteed year-round worker income, and
    B. Guaranteed annual wages within the industries is a proper and workable answer to this need.

THE NARRATIVE—CHRONOLOGICAL ORDER

Out Over Kicking Horse Pass

I. The trip was part of a long-planned summer in Canada
    A. We've all heard about seeing America first
        1. My friend Bob and I had already visited Mexico
        2. Had been by boat to Alaska
        3. Had touched in all but three of the states
        4. Had liked all of it.
    B. In 1948 we had finally reached Banff in the Canadian Rockies
        1. Found it one of the most magnificent mountain areas in the world
        2. But then someone told us we hadn't seen anything until we went out over Kicking Horse Pass. Bob was picture hungry
II. So we decided to go and I want to tell the consequences
    A. We decided to drive over and rough it a bit
        1. Took a tent and promised to use it
        2. Brought along cooking equipment and the food to cook in it
        3. Left everything sissy at Lake Louise
    B. We saw many interesting sights in the forenoon
        1. Natural bridge
        2. Mt. Eisenhower
        3. Glaciers
        4. Wild mountain sheep

   C. We camped at noon and went native
     1. Found tent-pitching no picnic but made it
     2. Found cooking over open fire messy
     3. But the results even messier
     4. Straightened camp after taking luggage from car
   D. We tried our hand at mountain climbing
     1. Picked Mt. Temple
     2. Walked over to its base — a two-hour jaunt that looked like ten minutes
     3. Started up as directed by hostile guide
     4. Nearly died before either would cry uncle
     5. Bob's nosebleed allowed us to quit with honor
     6. Spectacular thunderstorm and rain hit us on way down
   E. After that we had nothing but trouble
     1. Wet going slowed us — invited stone bruises
     2. We arrived in camp, after a lost spell, around 10:30 P.M.
     3. For some reason our tent had leaked
     4. Our change was from dripping wet clothes to merely soggy ones
     5. The fire wouldn't start
     6. Finally we threw things together and drove on
     7. Long hours later we turned in at a cabin camp at sunrise and slept until noon
III. The moral is probably this: Don't camp out — use the facilities.
    P.S. The pictures were great — and most people don't get the story with them.

THE INDUCTIVE PATTERN

From Winston Churchill's speech, *Europe in Suspense*, delivered in a broadcast message to the people of the United States on August 8, 1939, we have the following fine example of the inductive pattern.

   I. It was only last year the Nazis liberated Austria from the horrors of self-government.
  II. It was only in March they freed the Czechoslovak Republic from the misery of independent existence.

III. It is only two years ago that Signor Mussolini gave the ancient kingdom of Abyssinia its Magna Charta.

IV. It is only two months ago that little Albania got its writ of Habeas Corpus, and Mussolini sent in his Bill of Rights for King Zog to pay.

V. Why, even at this moment, the mountaineers of Tyrol, a German-speaking population who have dwelt in their beautiful valleys for a thousand years, are being *liberated*, that is to say, uprooted, from the land they love.

VI. From all these activities we must conclude that the fascist powers are bent on aggression and intend to continue it.

If you have a choice, and some one form of arrangement is not imperative, then your main concern becomes one of the order in which you will place your points. Here you might come up against the old argument about primacy versus recency. If you have a certain point which you are especially anxious to get across to your listener should it be handled first or should it come last in your speech? The more students of the psychology of learning work on this problem the less certain they are of the answer. In their second fight for the middleweight title Gene Fulmer and Ray Robinson suggested an answer to this question. Fulmer landed the first punch — and the next hundred, too, for that matter. In the fifth round you will remember Robinson landed a punch. It was delivered much later than the Fulmer blows but it was decisive. It was later but better. Here's the answer: It isn't decisive how early or how late a point is introduced in your speech. Much more important is how effectively it is presented.

"Introduction, body, and conclusion"

Every speech must begin somewhere, continue for some time, and end somewhere, but for the best results the introduction should be more than simply the place where the speaker starts talking. By the same token, the conclusion should be more than simply the point at which the speaker stops vocalizing. The introduction should be a carefully considered division of the speech. It should be designed to perform one or more of the following three functions: it should introduce the speaker to his listeners, it should introduce the subject to the listener, and/or it should set the mood of the audience. Many effective speakers, beginning with Cicero, have concentrated on the securing of personal acceptance in the opening remarks. They favor using the beginning of the speech for fixing an impression of their good will, authoritativeness, and sound character. If your reputation does not precede you or if you have not been introduced by another speaker in a separate speech, there is perhaps no better way to use the introduction. You may comment favorably on your listener or his community, reveal a shrewd knowledge of the prevailing interests in the audience or tell a revealing story about yourself.

If the speaker decides to use the introduction simply to acquaint the audience with his subject and purpose, he may decide that it is enough to begin directly with the topic sentence of the speech. If he feels no necessity for selling himself to the audience or trying to establish a mood, he may simply begin by saying, "I intend to talk to you for the next few minutes about . . . ," and then plunge right into the body of his speech. There are many situations in which a speaker is better off to cut out a lot of preliminary chatter and go right to the point. If advance analysis of the audience seems to call for it, the introduction may be used to set the mood of the audience. If, for example, you have reason to anticipate hostility, you will want to spend some time in working for a mood of agreement. If the audience is likely to be basically indifferent, introductory time may be spent wisely in establishing "rapport." Finally, whatever function you decide upon for your introduction, remember not to prepare it until you have pretty well completed the rest of your speech. After all, you can't introduce a speech you haven't even worked out yet.

No matter which of the earlier mentioned methods of arrangement you may decide to use in the body of the speech, the total effect should be one of compactness and logical consistency. The points should form a pattern and each point should be supported adequately. The sources of supporting material are treated elsewhere in this book and they should be drawn upon intelligently in the body of any speech.

The conclusion of a speech should provide an effect of finality. The speech should seem to end and not merely cease to continue. The audience should have a definite feeling that what you got up there to say has been said. Several types of conclusion are usually recognized; the kind used should be dictated by the kind of subject, the specific purpose, the audience, or the occasion. Perhaps the most frequently used is the summary. In this conclusion the speaker merely restates in concise language the points he has advanced. The method seems a little obvious to some speakers who feel that a short rehash of everything they have just said is a kind of reflection on the audience's intelligence. Experience indicates, however, that the average listener genuinely appreciates a summary both because it fortifies recall and because it provides an opportunity for a final check. If the purpose of your speech is to leave in mind a sequence of points or a process, you should summarize in conclusion. Somewhere I have come across the story of a seasoned advocate who was offering his prayers one night. After a few minutes he was heard to say, "And now, Lord, in conclusion, let me summarize. . . ."

Some speeches may better be concluded with a quotation. This quotation may be a particularly pointed statement by some authority which will give finality to the conclusion or it may be a passage of poetry or literary prose which will provide a kind of inspirational clincher to your remarks. Unfortunately too many speeches contain nothing of worth other than the concluding stanzas or paragraphs from the masters. Beware of concluding an utterly prosaic recital of facts with some uncalled-for passage from *The Psalm of Life, The Chambered Nautilus* or the *Ole Swimmin' Hole*. For better or worse, generations of audiences in this country have learned to identify the quotation of verse with a certain type of stale and profitless "inspirational oratory."

This long-continued abuse of intrinsically fine literary materials has practically destroyed their usefulness for speech purposes and you will probably be wise to avoid them.

Now that we have reviewed the three parts of a speech the following outline might serve as a useful reference. Keep it before you next time you are working on a talk.

Introduction

Personal appeals go well here

Has three functions. These are not necessarily all present in every speech.

1. It makes contact with the audience.
   a. By finding common ground.
   b. By giving audience a chance to get acquainted with the speaker.
2. It gets attention.
   a. By tie-in with preceding speaker, occasion, place, etc.
   b. By story.
   c. Through paradox or other striking statement.
   d. Through rhetorical question.
3. It states and limits the subject of the speech. It puts the idea in a topic sentence.

Body

Logical factual appeals fit here

(Sometimes called discussion)

1. It breaks down and arranges the idea.
   a. It presents the sub-points (rarely more than five).
   b. It arranges the sub-points in most effective order.
      1. Logical order — syllogism, inductive-deductive, causal.
      2. Chronological order — order of events, story.
      3. Conventional order — the way the topic is always treated.
      4. Positional order — left to right, top to bottom, etc.

Body

(*continued*)

      5. String-of-beads order — "accidental" order.

2. It develops the idea.
   a. By exposition.
   b. By narration.
   c. By description.
   d. By persuasion.

Conclusion

*Emotional-
motivational
appeals
belong here*

Has four functions
1. Summarizes ideas.
2. Applies ideas.
3. Moves to action on the ideas.
4. Epitomizes.

EXERCISES

Selecting points

1. You are preparing a ten-minute talk. Your purpose is to present your reasons for a reduction in the personal income tax. What points seem important to you? Jot down as many arguments for such a reduction as occur to you. When you have listed all the points that come to you, look them over. Are there any duplications? Are there some of these points that seem more important than others? Drop any arguments that aren't essential.

Now about the order of points. Does any order suggest itself? In other words is there one point that seems to you best for an opener? a clincher? Can you use a causal sequence to show that the tax should be cut? Is a problem-solution arrangement better?

2. You are going to sell a three-bedroom suburban home. You hope to get around thirty-five thousand dollars. A prospect is coming to talk over the property. Put down all the points that might be appealing to this prospect, in terms of what you know about him. What should you stress? The price? The location? The exterior construction? Materials? Arrangement of interior? In what order will you present these advantages? Is there anything you can safely leave out of your remarks unless it is called for by the prospect?

Introduction

1. In the aforementioned speech on income tax reduction what use will you make of your introduction? Will you tell the audience why *you* have taken it upon yourself to present these arguments? Will you give them reasons why you are especially well qualified to make these arguments? Does this audience need to be challenged to attention on the subject? Will a story come in handy as a starter? Is this a good situation in which to get right down to business with a simple statement of purpose and no other preliminaries?

2. Read or listen to several speeches. In terms of the outline on the functions of the Introduction on page 99, what does each speaker do? Does he do it well? Can you see ways in which he might have achieved his purpose better?

Conclusion

In terms of the functions of the Conclusion, what kind of materials would you use to end the speech on income tax reduction? What are the advantages of the summary for such a speech? Can you find a quotation conclusion that might be appropriate here? What about an appeal for action?

Turn to the speeches in Part Four. Note the conclusions used by these speakers. Evaluate them.

Find a sermon, a political speech, and a project report. Note the conclusion of each of these. Can you understand why each speaker used the materials he used in these speeches? Were the conclusions effective? Why? If they were not particularly good, can you tell why? Can you suggest improvements?

SUPPORTING MATERIALS

"Supporting materials come from many sources"

Having decided upon his specific purpose and having selected and arranged the points through which he intends to accomplish that purpose, the speaker comes next to the question of what to say in support of each of these points. Where does one find supporting materials? The traditional sources are the speaker's experience, conversation with others, and reading. Aristotle devoted a large part of a ponderous volume to invention — in other words, to the investigation and classification of the various sources of ideas. Cicero claimed the whole province of knowledge as the speaker's legitimate source of material. For our purposes, however, resources need not be so exhaustive. Although the speaker benefits directly from a wide background of information — a background extending well beyond his special field of interest — he may, if he is at all alert, speak with good results from his own background of experience, association, and reading. Don't minimize your own competence as a source of speech material. Don't take the attitude so often expressed that nothing interesting has ever happened to you. Every individual's life is distinctive and therefore potentially interesting. The way in which you have met problems, the evaluative judgments you have made, the ways in which you have reacted to universal experience will interest other people if given a chance.

Occasionally, of course, you will want to go beyond personal knowledge and experience and you may do this either by asking for the information and opinions of other people and then quoting them, or by looking up printed sources. Undoubtedly, the most widely used source is reading; and this is as it should be. After all, something pertinent and valid has been written upon almost every subject and the best thoughts of the race are available in print.

Any librarian will be glad to recommend sources of information in the specific field in which you are seeking material, if such sources as the card index, the *Readers' Guide*, *Who's Who*, and the *Encyclopædia Britannica* do not prove sufficient. If you are a busy speaker who confronts popular audiences frequently, you will do well to keep a notebook, and if you intend to talk intensively in a certain narrow field it is advisable that you build a card file on the subject, but such measures are not indicated for the casual and occasional speaker. In a very real sense, your whole life will prove to be preparation for any speech you are likely to make. Your vocational background, your cultural interests, your social environment, will find expression in what you say and in how you say it. The more interesting you are as a person the more interesting what you will have to say. Talk most about what you know best.

"The three areas of persuasion as sources of material"

The three general areas of persuasion provide a useful division of material along the lines of purpose. These three areas may be thought of as personal, logical-factual, and emotional-motivational. In other words, your materials may render you more acceptable to your audience, they may make your conclusion logically inescapable, or they may win acceptance through their appeal to some of the emotions. Let us consider these three areas separately.

"The materials of personal persuasion"

First, the personal. In a sense the speaker must become the spokesman of his audience. Whether as listener or speaker you have all been present at the time when a speaker has evidently won acceptance from an audience. This may be manifested in an increasingly uncritical attitude or even in a fondly possessive mood best characterized by the expression, "That's our boy!" This attitude in the audience is invaluable, and it is best achieved in three ways: by making the audience feel that the speaker likes them; that he knows what he is talking about; and that he is a person of good character. As we mentioned in Part One, *The Speaker*, these three impressions must be conveyed to the audience both through physical action and through selection of ideas. Hence, materials which impress upon the audience the good nature, intelligence, and reliability of the speaker are the proper subject matter of personal acceptability. The greatest short cut to desired results in speaking is the acceptance of the speaker as a good and reliable man by the listeners.

"Logical-factual materials"

Logical-factual materials are such materials as may be used to convince the listener. Such materials should prove beyond a reasonable doubt the truth of a certain statement or the advisability of a certain action. These may include syllogistic logic, causal reasoning, analogy and example, testimony, and statistics. Books have been written on logical argument, but for our purposes we may limit ourselves to the logical sequence known as the syllogism in which a specific case is related to a general truth and a conclusion is drawn. For example: (1) All Communists believe in the destruction of capitalism; (2) John Doe is a Communist; (3) therefore, John Doe believes in the destruction of capitalism. This deductive device is our most popular logical weapon. If you can discover a generally accepted truth for your first premise and relate a specific case to this first premise, then the listener is forced to the conclusion indicated. Such a method of making the point logically inescapable is very appealing, especially to people who pride themselves upon their use of reason. Unfortunately this logical sequence is subject to serious misuse. For example, it may be emotionalized, expressed with great fervor and emphasis, and turned to unfair purposes. If we take our above-mentioned syllogism, assume a hall full of excited Americans, jealous of individual liberties and rendered suspicious of all Reds, it is not hard to see the danger. A speaker might say, "All Communists believe in the destruction of capitalism. This John Doe goes around making nasty remarks about the capitalistic system. The man is obviously a Red." This, of course, is fallacious but it is not hard to conceive of the crowd making things mighty uncomfortable for the unfortunate Mr. Doe.

Another weakness of the logical sequence is that there is a remarkable dearth of generally accepted truths. Certain general statements may be used effectively as first premises in certain audiences when they would be totally unacceptable in others. A speaker might use the major premise, "Women are poor drivers," before an audience of men with resounding success. He could scarcely hope to get very far with it before an audience of women. Or take the premise: "All wage raises must be reflected in increased prices." This statement would be completely acceptable at the average managerial meeting, considerably less acceptable at union hall.

Causal reasoning is very useful to the speaker. This may be cause-to-effect, effect-to-cause, or effect-to-effect. When the connection is made from cause to effect you have examples like the following: If a man gets up in the morning and hears over the radio that the temperature was 10° below zero last night, he remembers with consternation that he forgot to put antifreeze in his car. He recognizes freezing as an effect of low temperature and he knows he is in trouble.

In the effect-to-cause process the same man may leave the house without having turned on his radio. When he sees ice on the pool beside the walk, he knows that the temperature was at least 32° F. during the night because, seeing a present effect, he relates it to a familiar cause.

In the effect-to-effect process, seeing the ice on the pool, the man knows without going to the garden that his tomato plants are wilted. From the one present effect he deduces another usual effect.

The dangers in the use of causal relationships are these: The avowed cause may not be sufficient to produce the assumed effect, the effect claimed may be produced by other causes, or circumstances may be such as to prevent the usual effect. I have in mind here a speech that I heard several times in the period when America was debating the policy of compulsory military training. The speaker, an opponent of such a policy, reviewed the history of the past two wars. He identified the Germany of World War I as a nation with an elaborate military training program. Germany was beaten at that time by nations with untrained armies. Again Germany had compulsory training prior to World War II — indeed there was only one Western European nation with a bigger trained army. That was France. In Asia Japan had taken over the compulsory training idea on a larger scale. What happened? The biggest pre-trained force, that of France, collapsed without a struggle; the next, that of Germany, again folded in the face of drafted armies. In Japan another long-term training program failed to produce. The point made by our speaker was this: The best guarantee of ultimate defeat in war is a program of compulsory military training in peacetime! Here you have a use of causal argument that seems not to ring true. One suspects that other causes were operative, that other factors entered into the downfall of the trained nations. Lack of economic strength, faulty strategy, and lack of size are only a few of the other possibilities.

In the selection of materials it is wise to avoid these hasty assumptions of causal relationship. Look over very carefully any cause or sign before you accept it as proof. Once you have found valid causal arguments, however, you have powerful and persuasive materials for your purpose.

"Examples and analogies are persuasive"

Examples and analogies are perhaps the most widely used of supporting materials. The function of examples is, of course, inductive, but it is extremely improbable that the average speaker with the average limitations of time can provide a sufficient number of examples to satisfy the demands of scientific induction. In a speech of from twenty minutes to an hour in length — in other words, in any you are likely to make — you will be limited to a selection of comparatively few examples. These examples must be chosen carefully because of their emotional impact, pertinence, and conclusiveness. For the purposes of the speaker, two or three examples must suffice.

Several years ago when the postwar plight of Europe was still great, two speakers talked at a Midwest meeting to raise funds for relief. One of them dealt strictly in figures. In Poland one million people on the verge of starvation. In Hungary a total population existing on a food supply estimated at about one-fifth of minimum need, etc. There was no effort to dramatize the figures, grim as they were. The second speaker really did the job, as far as the fund-raising was concerned. He gave some of the figures, too, but what affected the audience most powerfully was his vivid word picture of children and old folks digging around in the garbage cans and eagerly munching on such refuse as they could find there.

The power of examples should not be ignored in less dramatic situations. The Caterpillar Tractor Company uses figures from several large turnpike construction jobs to show both the preponderant use of their equipment, and the relative efficiency of that equipment from the maintenance standpoint. This material in the hands of a salesman is bound to be effective, because specific examples give the prospect something to go by — something tangible to use as a basis for decision.

While arguing the question of continued economic aid for foreign countries, advocates of large cuts in such aid have never been more persuasive than when they turn to examples. When heavy tractors are sent to rice paddies and dams are built where there is no water the listener can lay hold on the problem of waste. It takes a lot of long-range-need argument to offset such specific present cases. Even one example which is exactly right is worth more than a perfunctory recital of eight or ten instances in establishing a conclusion in the minds of the audience.

Analogies, or similar instances, should be selected so that they have significant identity with the case under consideration. If they are literal analogies, they must have more points in common than points of difference. For example, if one presents the liquor licensing system used by the State of Illinois as an argument for a similar liquor licensing system in New Mexico, one must be sure that there are not too many differences in population, racial background, income level, and religion. If too many of these points of difference immediately suggest themselves, the effect of the analogy will be small.

Britain and the United States are both basically democratic nations and have long been so. When you can find something political that works among British people and suggest this as proof that it will work among Americans you are on pretty solid ground. The parliamentary form of government with its combination of the legislative and administrative functions has often been seriously recommended for the United States. But the suggestion that our democratic form of government would solve all the problems of the Russian people may need a little more documentation. There are those who feel that the Russian people simply are not ready for such a change. It might confuse or even irritate them.

Aside from the literal analogy, the speaker may use the formal analogy. Sometimes these imaginative parallels are surprisingly effective. I suppose there is no formal analogy as widely known in America as the Lincoln comment on swapping horses in midstream. This has been offered seriously as an excuse for remaining at midstream almost indefinitely by a number of politicians and administrators in our time. Most often the formal analogy comes in the form of a proverb. You will recognize "Birds of a feather flock together," "Too many cooks spoil the broth," and the like. A considerable reach must be made by the listener in the best of these analogies and their success depends a great deal upon just the right touch of good humor. Formal analogies should always be delivered with a smile.

"Quotation of authorities is a form of support"

In the logical-factual area, one of the most popular forms of support is the testimony of authorities. Scarcely a persuasive speech of any length is delivered without at least one quotation. This quotation from the writing or remarks of an alleged authority in the field is employed to fortify statements of fact or opinion used by the speaker. Expert opinion is, of course, strongly persuasive. The ordinary individual is not in a position, for example, to quarrel with the economic theories of a trained economist, and the court of law must accept the judgment of fingerprint experts. This recognition of the special validity of expert witness leads to certain abuses by speakers. For example, you have all heard quotations from well-known scientists, distinguished business leaders, and famous surgeons. Perhaps you yourself have so labeled certain of your authorities. Such vague identifications should leave the listener completely unimpressed, and even though there is no doubt that some people are sufficiently gullible to accept them, they are scarcely ever worth using. Try to be sure that the special authoritativeness of the man you are quoting is well known to your audience.

This leads us to a second danger in the quoting of authorities which we shall call the transfer of authority. Lacking quotable big names in the special field under consideration, the speaker is strongly tempted to quote from men who are unmistakably in the public eye in some other field. Human nature being what it is, there is no lack of dogmatic statement outside of their own field of special authority by various big-shots. Hence, we have the phenomenon of men who have achieved a happy combination of the internal combustion engine and a four-wheel wagon delivering dicta on racial discrimination and international diplomacy, and men who may or may not be distinguished surgeons from Vienna rendering pronouncements on deodorants and mouth wash. It is well for the speaker to remember that this trap is laid for him when he is on the trail of supporting materials.

There are, of course, some official positions which bring along with them a certain authoritativeness. The President of the United States, for instance, has an ex-officio authority in many fields, and this is as it should be since the supreme executive either possesses or has access to a wider range of information than most of us can hope for. Similar reliability is usually associated with the remarks of college presidents and top business administrators.

Another requirement in the use of authority in a speech is that of quotability. Unfortunately, many a man of unimpeachable authority has gone on record in such drab and unintelligible jargon, that to quote him may be the best way to lose audience interest and attention. You as a speaker must make your own decision between greater authority and greater quotability.

On one last point about quoted material, let us consider a story. I once heard a speaker in an attempt to cast doubt on a certain monetary policy under debate, read a statement from an economics treatise, as follows: "It is almost unbelievable that any experts in finance would ever endorse such a proposal." This sounded fine. Unfortunately for the quoter, however, a member of the opposition had the same book. He finished the quotation — it went like this: "nevertheless many of them do endorse it." Be careful not to quote out of context. Get the exact passage and get all of it.

Concise and forceful statements by authorities are among the strongest of supporting materials. Use them, but use them sparingly, being careful to avoid turning your speech into a mere collection of quotations.

The Saturday Evening Post

"THESE ARE NOT MY OWN FIGURES I'M QUOTING. THEY'RE THE
FIGURES OF SOMEONE WHO KNOWS WHAT HE'S TALKING ABOUT."

"Figures need not lie"

Statistical evidence is, of course, a form of example but it
looms so large in speaking for results that it deserves at least brief
special consideration here. It has been said that Americans tend
to worship statistical averages. This is the land where every
family has two and two-thirds children, lives in one-fourth of a
house with two and one-fifth bedrooms and six-eighths of a bath-
room, and drives three-fourths of a car. All of us have heard
that figures don't lie but liars unfortunately do figure, and that

there are three degrees of falsehood — lies, damned lies, and statistics. Despite these expressions of skepticism, we are still impressed with figures, and a speaker who fails to employ them is depriving himself of one of our strongest persuasive forces.

There are, however, certain precautions which should be kept in mind in the use of statistics in a speech. First, the speaker should remember that exhaustive figures are likely to be exhausting figures. Since only a mathematical genius can hold in mind intelligently any considerable sequence of numbers, and most listeners soon reach the saturation point in the assimilation of statistics, the speaker should use figures very sparingly; and the figures which he does use should be chosen for their impact and ease of recall. If you find yourself in a position where a lot of figures must be left with the audience, get them mimeographed or printed in a comprehensive form and have them distributed to your audience. Then present a few of the most striking figures from the floor and spend most of your time making sure that the printed figures will be read later. Bearing in mind the necessity for maintaining respect for his knowledge and integrity, the speaker should ask himself the following questions before he uses statistics in a speech. Have the figures been checked for absolute accuracy? Has there been a sufficient sampling taken? Have the figures been rendered emotionally unacceptable to your particular listener?

The first two of these questions should need no elaboration. The last is one that many a speaker has failed to answer to his regret. It simply means that statistics showing the rarity of death by lightning, impressive as they are, will carry little weight with the survivors of a man who has just been killed by lightning.

"Man needs more than a reason"

The third general area of persuasion — the emotional-motivational — has already been covered in a section on the listener in Part Two. Materials which set in motion the basic drives and which are selected for special motive appeals must play a large part in speaking for results. Although it is possible for the speaker to confine himself almost entirely to emotional appeal in a speech, such appeals are usually found to stem from logical-factual materials, as we have already indicated. These appeals cannot be kept out of the severest logical sequences and the most objective of statistical presentations.

Something should be said about the ethics of appeal at the emotional level. Some people profess to scorn such appeals. Most of us, indeed, consider ourselves to be products of the age of reason and we like to view with contempt purely emotional responses. As a result of this prevailing attitude, many speakers try to avoid or perhaps try to appear to avoid materials aimed at the basic drives. This is unrealistic and quite uncalled for. It is pretty evident that the listener responds all over and that, being a human being, he always will. Your speaking produces not only mental reactions but emotional and physical reactions. These are not separable. It is demonstrable that the speaker, when he produces any positive responses at all, produces just as definite visceral and muscular responses as so-called mental. It would seem then that the speaker who is after results will ignore the artificial distinction made in favor of mental response and will deal with his listeners as human beings. If he wishes to control the opinions and actions of people, he will appeal frankly to their feeling as well as to their thinking.

"Visual aids must be visible and must aid"

Among the materials available to the speaker in almost every field these days, visual aids must have a prominent place. Add films and television to the time-honored graph, chart, picture, and exhibit and we have indeed a formidable body of helpful materials.

If you use graphs or charts be careful to have them printed or drawn large enough to be seen by all to whom they will be shown. How large this will be depends upon the size and arrangement of the room. If the group is small you may invite them to gather around up front. If the crowd is a large one with people placed in rows and pretty well settled for the duration of the meeting, you must get bigger and clearer figures. As for what goes on the graphic displays the same rules apply here as would apply in book illustrations. The card should be uncluttered, with the printed matter reduced to absolute essentials. Contrasts must be achieved unmistakably through varieties of color or shape of figure. Most of the readers will be able to get needed materials for graphic use quite easily. Be sure they're in just the right size and form before taking them to your listeners.

Pictures, either painting or photograph, are of very little use before groups of any size unless they are available for passing around, or can be projected from slides. To use a picture from the platform can be futile and irritating. I should think that perhaps the most useless application of this type of alleged aid is this one from my undergraduate days. Our earnest professor opened a duodecimo volume at the frontispiece, flashed it at us from the lectern and said, "I know you probably can't see it from there, but this is a likeness of William Shakespeare." It could have been a portrait of Mickey Mouse for all we could see, and the professor knew it. He admitted it yet couldn't resist the fatal temptation to *show* us something. Perhaps he had read somewhere that one picture is worth a thousand words, a timeworn truism that depends for its validity upon the picture and the words under consideration.

Demonstrating equipment before the group or incorporating graphs, charts or pictures in your talk calls for a bit of special advice. Don't huddle with your materials on blackboard or chart rack. We once had a line coach who added a touch of mystery to his chalk sessions on football. He'd plot a defensive line-up on the board and while talking about it he would move up on the little line of x's and o's and interpose about four feet of All-American back and shoulder between the worried tackles and guards and next Saturday's plays. You might not have the muscle that coach had — but the bulk can be there. Keep out of your own and your audience's way while using visual aids. If you are so placed that you are always blocking the view for a part of your group, be sure to shift sides from time to time so that all parts of the crowd can keep up.

Now about films. Much excellent film is available, and it can be a tremendous help to you whether it accompany promotional talks, informational speeches or policy discussions. Much of this film may be obtained at a minimal charge from university services or public libraries. You may even have some of your own photography that you can use on film to good advantage. Motion pictures function as a kind of "deep freeze" unit where experience and action can be set aside at will for future use as needed. More often than not processes may be better learned through a combination of films and oral comment than through the most lucid of straight oral explanation.

As a parting word on visual aids, be warned against using them just to be using them. These "through the eye" devices are enjoying a wide popularity today that amounts almost to a fad. Don't go out and find something visual just from the feeling that anybody who's anybody must bring at least a projector along on every speech occasion. Not more than a year ago I was seated in a dark room with a group of young insurance executives watching a movie on "How to Conduct a Meeting." Suddenly it came to me that there was something wrong with the set-up. Why should a trained instructor with a group of alert students be sitting in darkness watching another man with the same kind of group doing what we ought to be doing ourselves. We turned on the lights and had our own parliamentary session where we learned to do by doing — and very likely learned conduct of a meeting better than we could have learned it by watching pictures of other people doing it. Be sure your visual aids are really needed before you use them.

"It's not easy to be funny"

"I've been asked to talk at the meeting tomorrow and I have to find a good joke." Ever hear that one? It points up the whole problem of humor in speaking. Everybody seems to feel this unshakable confidence in humor, everybody accepts the idea that if he can find a good joke or a wisecrack or two his speaking difficulties are over. And humorous materials are of great importance in speechmaking. It is possible that they have been a bit overrated in some circles, but they are sufficiently valuable to merit our special consideration here.

First, humor must be judged by the result it achieves. That result is, of course, amusement. But amusement seems to take many forms. It also occurs at many levels. The difference between the raucous spasm we identify as the "belly laugh" and the quiet smile signaling our appreciation of some neat irony or subtle jibe may well be one of kind as well as degree. Still we know when we are amused and perhaps that is enough. For speech purposes humorous devices may be divided into two classes: the witticism and the joke.

The wisecrack, the witty saying, is a hard thing to master. In fact in a book such as this, where the purpose is to make helpful suggestions or none at all, the temptation is great to dismiss the witty phrase with the comment that either you have the flair for it or you don't, and that if you don't have it nothing can be done about it. Let me compromise. Study yourself before giving up this form of humor. Since the neat turn of language depends upon a wide and flexible vocabulary, you can't be sure that you are permanently doomed to remain among the unamusing until you have worked at your supply of words along the lines set forth in Chapter 3. Find some understanding listener and try for an amused reaction from him. Remember the element of surprise, either in choice of words or in arrangement of words; the double meaning; the startlingly apt simile. Of these things witty speech is made. If you don't improve this way you might well listen and jot down such expressions as seem to you to be good, memorize them and work them into your speech. I feel sure that many a man with a reputation as a wit leans pretty heavily on this method if the truth were known.

As to the other common form, the joke, we can prescribe a bit more hopefully. I don't know who invents jokes, but this much is sure — few of our most successful humorous speakers work out their own. To put it another way, the jokes you tell need not be your own. I doubt that I can name the author of any of my old favorites, jokes I have used for years and have taken into my repertoire as if they were my own. Look for jokes. Whenever you hear a good one put it down in a notebook. Read the popular funny pages of papers and magazines, read the works of well-known storytellers, past and present. Don't even shun the joke books.

A note of warning here: Don't forget to clean house on your supply of anecdotes from time to time. Toss out the weatherbeaten items as they become used up and keep a fresh supply coming in. After years in the classroom, I am not so sure that the jibes at professors' oft-told stories are funny. There is a temptation, once you have come up with a good yarn, to keep it around too long, and I fear that college professors aren't the only ones who succumb to it.

The selection of humorous materials involves more than a quick glance through the funny pages and the book of jokes. You might profit from an analysis of the materials of humor.

We have already identified the two media for humor — the clever remark and the anecdote. Some people combine the two successfully, telling the story with little witty asides.

There are several kinds of witty remark. Consider the gentle touch — funny but not at all mean. This includes the observation, almost in proverb form, that one can pick up in most of the popular periodicals. An example will serve: There is some doubt as to the biggest building in the world, but there's no doubt about the biggest room in the world — it's the room for improvement.

The witticism may be quite sharp. Centuries ago Cicero, disgusted with the pompous posturing of his son-in-law who had just become an army officer, pointed him out as "the little man over there — the one attached to the sword." The sharp remark is brilliantly exemplified in our times in the series called "The Perfect Squelch," appearing in the *Saturday Evening Post.*

What about sarcasm? Let's begin by admitting that stinging sarcasm can be very amusing — for everyone but the object of the attack. I am not one who believes that many delicate, budding personalities have been permanently distorted and many lives ruined by sarcasm. My objection to bitter wisecracking is that unless the bystander is a rare character indeed he will cringe even while he laughs as you flay somebody else. He won't be able to get out of his mind how he would feel if the knife were turned upon him. A kind of nervous admiration is about all you can hope for from sarcasm. Avoid it unless the occasion allows for the half-serious give-and-take that we call repartee. This, of course, can be fun.

The remark may be in the dead-pan category and be very effective. Some of our best entertainers have specialized in comments that were so dumb they were funny. Take the story of the drunk who fell from a third floor window and hit on the walk below. As the crowd rushed up to him a policeman yelled, "What happened here?" The drunk sat up and said, "I don't know, officer, I just got here myself."

Be sure that your story is new. If it's any good and does not originate with you, it's too much to hope that no one in your audience has heard it, but try to be sure that very few have. If you tend to personalize your stories, that is, if you tell them as if they happened to you, the necessity for newness is even more important. Try to relate your story to the rest of your speech. Many speakers — some of them fairly successful — consider a good story an end in itself, but there will always be a sufficient number of chronically cynical listeners who will resent being entertained to no purpose. Perhaps it would be well to end this advice with a story. Several years ago a college professor of my acquaintance made a speech before the students and faculty of a small high school. The *pièce de resistance* of his offering was a story. It was all too evidently a dud. Immediately after the

speech a young teacher who as yet had not made the nice adjustment between honesty and tact came forward and said, "Prof,
there were two reasons why the kids didn't laugh at your yarn
today. First, there was a speaker here last week who told the
same story; and second, he told it better than you did."

"The story will make your point"

In Chapter 5 we have considered the narrative as an attention-getter. The story does a lot more than gain attention and
provide relief from the strain of listening, however. As mentioned earlier, Jesus relied heavily on the story to make a point.
You will remember the story of the good Samaritan. This was
an unadorned tale, free from moralizing elaboration. It needed
no flourishes — no interpretation. It argued more strongly than
any logical sequence. It was all the answer needed to the question, "Who is my neighbor?"

Often the speaker scurries about in search of just the right
argument, the right set of figures, the exact quotation, when all
the time a story is at hand that would do the job better than any
of these. Lew Sarett, great teacher of persuasion, used to say
that only the inexperienced speechmaker neglected the narrative
form as a source. Seasoned speakers often turn to it.

Not only does the story lay hold upon attention and make
the point. It may also provide the only means of presenting certain ideas without offense since it has just the right flavor of in-
directness. In this connection the publisher of a daily reminder
sheet devoted to advertising moved a large group of non-
subscribing readers of his paper into buying their own copies.
He published a little story of what happened to a fictitious character who acquired a permanent kink in his neck as a result
of his innocent habit of staring over other people's shoulders.
Many of the offenders who hadn't responded at all to direct appeals and scoldings, chuckled over the story, got the point, and
good-naturedly shelled out the price.

"You can get there from here"

Direction, explanation, and description are important to the speaker. There is a real point behind the old story of the hillbilly who finally despaired of directing the outsider to Jake Smith's place across the valley and said, "I tell yuh, Mister, yuh jest cain't git there from here." There is no tougher test of oral communication than the task of giving directions. If you doubt the difficulty be sure to try the experiment recommended in the exercises at the end of this chapter. I once promised to grade a group of engineering students strictly on the ease with which I could get down to the largest department store in a neighboring city by following directions they gave in a classroom speech. Several of them tried to send me in the wrong direction down one-way streets, some failed to mention intervening streets, two forgot dead ends. Considering how much we deal in direction-giving, explaining and describing, most of us are remarkably bad at doing these things. A bit of briefing on the materials and methods involved seems in order.

It is a widely accepted fact among sales people that explanation sells. Much of the time a good explanation of how the product works is all that is needed to convince the buyer. The virtues of the policy or system are usually made most clear by simple explanation of how they operate. Observe how the car salesman, even though not neglecting beauty of line and luxury of appointments, still stresses the functional side of his car. He tells us how it works, and why it works better than others.

Unfortunately, however, much of the explanation one hears is sketchy, scattered, and ineffective. What are the characteristics of good explanation? First, the process to be explained must be studied carefully. It must be fully understood by the person doing the explaining. Second, the process must be outlined with each step in its proper time order. Failure to put first things first weakens the listeners' grasp of the process. Third, clear, exact language is essential here. There is no place for fine language in explanation. The lyrical passages should be saved for the end of the explanation when your purpose is to praise the process, if it is necessary then. Good explanation creates a strong interest of itself. It scarcely ever needs any fortification.

A program you wish to have adopted may best be presented to your listeners by explaining how it will work. An audience that sees the advantages of your proposal in terms of what it will do when put into effect will more readily give it their support.

"Descriptive materials can be influential"

You will observe from the material on explanation that the car salesman also makes use of description. He knows that color and line, stainless steel, and rich interiors are more powerfully persuasive with some prospects than such intangibles as careful construction and operational efficiency. Industrial engineers have often admitted regretfully that better machines can be built, from the purely functional standpoint, than the buying public will accept. Sales people have decided that spectacular visual appeals will sell more of almost anything from houses to perambulators, than will functional efficiency and durability. Well-done description can be effective with more than the frivolous and gullible, however. A report on the materials used is also descriptive and can prove very influential with a segment of your audience that isn't particularly responsive to eye-catchng beauty.

How shall one describe well? In the first place good description, like good explanation, can only come from thorough knowledge of the thing described. Know all the important facts about the person or thing you intend to present. Second, careful analysis of the potential listener must precede presentation. Third, you will work out an outline that gives ample coverage to all important points described. Finally, the language of descriptive speech has certain characteristics. It must convey images — be vivid. Use language that tells what the described subject is like as to form, color, sound, touch. See the section on vivid language in Chapter 3.

EXERCISES

Sources of speech materials

1. You find it necessary to deliver a talk on recent industrial development in Canada. You have no background in experience for such a talk. List the sources you would use for getting the needed information.

2. Analyze a recent speech. What are the sources of information utilized by the speaker? What materials come from his own background? Is there anything from quoted authorities? Can you trace any of the materials to printed sources, such as professional publications, periodicals, encyclopedias?

Logical materials

1. Frame a syllogism for proof that we should have federal aid to education. What generally accepted truth can you start with? Experiment with this; try several sequences.

2. Reduce the following to a syllogism: Roger Something, the leading movie actor, wears Extra-special shirts. You too should wear shirts of this brand. Evaluate the logic.

3. You have asked someone if he thinks a certain applicant for an engineering position would be a good man. He answers with a question, "Well, he comes from California Tech, doesn't he?" Reduce this to a syllogism. Is the logic acceptable?

4. Examine the following major premises. Which are valid? Which are fallacious?

All women are poor car drivers.
All birds can fly.
All men are mortal.
All farmers need federal subsidies.
All Americans are friendly.
All Englishmen are humorless.
All professors are absent-minded.
All income should be taxed.
All horses have hooves.
All snails are slow moving.

Make a list of five generally accepted truths from which one could safely argue.

Factual materials

1. Prepare an example of each of the following: cause-effect, effect-effect, and effect-cause. Find examples of each of these in the current periodicals.

2. Find a good analogous case to support the proposal that the United States should legalize gambling. That Illinois should adopt an income tax.

3. You are making a case for annuity purchase. Find five examples which lend support to the idea that annuities are a good thing.

4. You are trying to interest a customer in buying common stocks. Select certain stocks and work up statistical proof. Check the figures for applicability and sufficient sampling.

Authorities

1. Find examples of transfer of authority, the "eminent surgeon from Vienna" technique, inarticulate authority, and quoting out of context.

2. Find at least two contemporary speeches in which the quotation of sound and powerful authority was decisive.

Visual materials

1. Prepare charts or graphs to accompany a speech on one of the following subjects:

A budget report   A building cost report

2. Prepare pictorial materials to use with a talk on one of the following:

The topography of Vermont
Modern art trends
My house

3. Prepare demonstrating materials for an explanatory talk on one of the following:

How to grill a steak
How to refinish an antique table

123

How to arrange a table centerpiece
How to operate a tape-recorder

4. Check on sources of film to accompany a discussion of modern life in the Netherlands. Work out a set of comments to go along with the pictures.

5. Watch a film on some industry (many are available). Evaluate it in terms of interestingness, accuracy, pertinence, organization, and overall adequacy. Can you suggest any ways in which the film might be improved?

Humor

1. Find a joke for use in each of the following areas:

Family meals	Mother-in-law
Top brass	Speechmaking
The dumb student	Hunting
Adolescent romance	Women's clothes

2. Try for the light touch in commenting on each of the following situations:

A boss calls a chronically late employee on the carpet.
A suitor is kept waiting an hour overtime by his young lady.
A group of fishermen are caught on a posted lake.
A middle-aged man goes ice skating.
A practical joker is caught in a "backfire."
An uninformed critic is confronted by a piece of modern painting.
A proud parent holds forth on the accomplishments of the wonder child.

Explanation and Description

1. Assume that you are at some point near the outskirts of your city. A stranger has asked directions for driving to some well-known building downtown. Try your hand at giving him good, clear directions. Does a map help?

2. You have been asked to instruct someone on how to assemble a vegetable dicer. Use demonstration with this one.

3. You have been asked how to use the index volume of an encyclopedia. Using the volume, show how to find materials on deciduous trees.

SUPPORTING MATERIALS

4. Describe without visual aids any one of the current cars. After you have done this try the same subject with the aid of colored pictures of the automobile.

5. Select the expressions in the following list that seem to you best for description. Why do you like them? What is wrong with the others?

classy	rocket-like	terrific
sizzling	inexpensive	silky
rich	give-away	bony
beautiful	peculiar	slender
powerful	weird	purring
sleek	exotic	cheap
mighty	odd	bookish
streamlined	air stream	raucous
slick	soft	smart
fine	smooth	great
pretty good	nice	tricky
wonderful	not bad	sound

Compare your choices with those of others who have looked at the list. Talk over the differences.

Part Four

Typical Speech Situations

The average man in business and the professions finds himself called upon many times to make speeches and participate in conferences. In a sense, each speech occasion is distinct from all that have gone before or are likely to follow, and it is a little dangerous to generalize and list types of speech. Nevertheless, there are certain characteristic situations for which the average person might as well prepare himself. This section of our book will present several such situations and make recommendations which have been found useful. It should be remembered, of course, that the following assignments do not pertain necessarily to separate speeches. For instance, the speaker may find it necessary to secure good will, to explain a process, to tell a story and to sell — all in the same speech. For purposes of advice and practice, however, the following units will be found most helpful.

1 TO SELL OR PROMOTE

OCCASION: Before listeners who are potential customers or prospective supporters.

DESIRED RESPONSE: The listener will buy or will commit himself to support.

METHODS: Set forth the product or project in its best possible light and at the same time intensify the prospect's felt need for it. This latter may be done by appealing to basic human drives, habits or needs. It must, however, be done in such a way that the listener first recognizes the need as being his own. The method of suggestion is most useful right here.

The single most persuasive factor is something worth while to sell. The mere explanation of something which fills a long-felt need is actually enough in most situations. Hence get your descriptive and explanatory materials clearly set up. What are the good things — the new features of your product? Get them clearly before the prospect. Use striking language, and relate your ideas to things that are well known to listeners. The Caterpillar Company, in its sales material, speaks of the precision of its crankshafts as follows: "Swiss watch makers advertise precision of 39 millionths of an inch. Precision on our crankshafts is from 8 to 20 times closer." Notice, that although most of us have no real concept of millionths of an inch, we are all familiar with the Swiss watch as an accepted symbol of precision work.

In most fields the era of one-shot sales is gone, if it was ever here. Today you sell the product, continuing service, long-range advice, and permanent interest in the buyer all in one package. If you are interested in insurance, for example, you will find that the policy-holders have bought, along with the policy, the services of a counselor. This approach should be stressed in your speaking. Work out materials that make the relationship between you and the prospect vivid. A good example is this one used in the Sentinel Press publication, "Your Estate."

THE VALUE OF A CO-PILOT IN ESTATE PLANNING

The presence of a co-pilot in the control cabin of a transport plane is a familiar safeguard. A large airliner represents an investment of several million dollars and there is the safety of the passengers to be considered. No modern airline would permit a passenger plane to leave the ground without a pilot and a co-pilot, each capable of handling the ship for the duration of the flight.

When the experienced hand of the owner of an estate is removed by death, the importance of adequate safeguards to keep it on an even keel and steer it safely through financial rough weather and economic storms is a highly important consideration. Indeed, failure to provide adequate controls and safeguards may have serious effects on the estate when the owner dies.

The stress of high federal and state taxes and lack of experienced guidance often wrecks substantial estates, leaving the heirs a depleted inheritance and a substantially reduced income. According to newspaper reports, many formerly large estates were reduced to a fraction of their original value after the owner died because there had been few or no plans made to safeguard it for the benefit of the heirs.

Through estate planning, the owner introduces the principle of a co-pilot into his estate, and his knowledge, skill and experience carry on to assure his family financial safety and an adequate income. Through careful planning the owner safeguards his estate and avoids possible serious shrinkage owing to state and federal taxes, administration expenses and other transfer costs.

As a rule it is a good idea to stress the positive approach in selling. There is less and less of the dramatic word picture of the poor housewife struggling with ancient and inefficient equipment in her kitchen as a prelude to sale. More and more the home freezer is heralded for its own merits, and as a means for making the good life even better. Car agents preface their remarks with, "Of course, there are a lot of fine cars on the market, but. . . ." As someone has put it, "You don't have to run down products X and Y to sell product Z."

Some Don'ts

Don't forget to give them the facts.
Don't forget to be ready to listen part of the time.
Don't forget the persuasiveness of description and explanation.
Don't overlook the effectiveness of concession.
Don't forget to ask for action.

The following is a fine example of the speech to promote and win support.

WHY SUPPORT THE NEW BOND ISSUE

Dr. W. Norman Wampler
Superintendent of Schools
Bellflower, California

Why Are We Here? It is my pleasure tonight to welcome you to the offices of the Bellflower Public Schools. Education in Bellflower and nationally is today facing many critical problems. Education is public business and, as such, is the concern of every citizen of our community. Our Board of Education desires, when faced with the necessity of making decisions of paramount importance, that those decisions represent the best thinking of the great majority of the total population. You people tonight represent thirty-five community groups. For the most part you are presidents of civic and fraternal organizations of our city. We know that you, particularly, want to make our community the best possible and hence our desire to take you into our confidence concerning an educational problem of paramount importance.

Emotional appeals. Pride and community spirit. Why you people are being talked to.

131

What Are Our Schools Greatest Needs? Many problems are facing education today. I would like to mention two at this time. One is our tremendous teacher shortage. A hundred thousand teachers left the profession during the war period. A majority of them entered industry or the armed services. For the most part they have not returned to the teaching profession. At the same time enrollment in teacher-training institutions was reduced almost to the vanishing point. The years since the close of the war have not brought a marked return of enrollment in our teaching-training institutions. Concurrently with the war period, also, has come an unprecedented increase in the birthrate. It is interesting to note that in Los Angeles County alone the birthrate in 1935 was 12 per thousand whereas in 1947 it was 24.4 per thousand. Furthermore, California, and particularly Southern California, is experiencing the greatest migration of people in all history. We are receiving thousands of new immigrants each month and their children must be educated. Thus, the teacher shortage problem, serious everywhere in the United States, is peculiarly acute here. We haven't time tonight to discuss possible solutions of the teacher shortage. Certainly, greater status for teachers, a greater sense of security, and higher financial rewards are important approaches to a solution.

It is of another problem, however, that I wish particularly to speak this evening. This second problem is allied with the first. It may be called our School Housing Crisis. I have mentioned the tremendous surge in our birthrate and the unique immigration movement into California. These two factors are largely responsible for our critical school building shortages.

Why Does Bellflower Face a Crisis in School Housing? Much could be said about school building as a

Good start on the general problem

Now to the specific problem

132

national problem, but may we look at our local situation for a few minutes? Our problem is particularly significant at the elementary school level because it is there that the increased birthrate is beginning to be felt in our schools. In 1940 there were but 1400 pupils in the elementary schools of Bellflower. Then came the war. Our two major airplane plants were built, and a host of other industries came into the Los Angeles area. Now in 1948 our elementary enrollment has reached four thousand. By looking at figures available with the Bureau of Vital Statistics we can estimate with considerable accuracy what our enrollment will be in the years just ahead. Accepting these figures and estimating our immigration increase rather conservatively at 5 per cent annually, we have estimated elementary school enrollment in Bellflower at six thousand for the year 1952.

How successfully are we housing these pupils? Well, you know the answer and it isn't a pleasant one. We were fortunate in securing Federal assistance during the war and erected five buildings during that period. We have just completed another elementary building this spring. Nevertheless, we still have thirty classes on half-day session. Since almost surely our enrollment will continue to mount at a figure approximating five hundred pupils annually, we must of necessity construct a sizable building each year in order to prevent our problem from becoming accentuated.

What Can We Do About It? Obviously, we must have more school buildings and we must have them quickly. Unfortunately, they will cost money, and a lot of money. Our buildings completed in the early years of the war were made available at a cost not greater than $6 per square foot. School buildings being finished in Southern California today are costing approximately $12 per square foot. With a

Here we come to the solution

thousand square feet needed for each classroom, and a great deal more needed for offices and cafeterias and corridors, the cost of any building is appalling.

Our present Educational Law Code provides that a school district may bond itself up to 5 per cent of its assessed valuation for the purpose of constructing schools. Our bond issue of 1945 exhausted most of our legal bonding capacity. On the basis of our present taxable valuation, we can legally vote an additional $375,000 in bonds. Such an amount would give us one average size elementary school building housing five hundred students. We would have no funds for inevitable growth. We have no resources for building the ten cafeterias now so badly needed at ten different elementary buildings now in existence and we would have no funds available for the central administration building which is a "must" in our over-all school house planning.

Fortunately, the State of California has taken cognizance of the need which exists in so many communities of our State. Legislation put into effect a year ago provides that when and if a school district exhausts its bonding capacity it may then petition the state for a subsidy to supplement its building program. Fifty-five million dollars were made available from state sources for this purpose. The sum is far from adequate to meet all the state's needs. Under present allocation procedures, districts are being given just enough subsidy to take care of present enrollments. Nothing is being made available at this time for anything other than classrooms. Nevertheless, we would profit materially by making ourselves eligible for state subsidy.

As I have indicated, we can have access to these state funds only through one procedure and that is by voting a bond issue of approximately $375,000. It is to get your reaction concerning this possibility that we have called you here tonight. We feel this is your problem as much as ours. None

Adroit use of statistics and other factual materials

of us enjoy paying taxes. A $375,000 bond issue will increase the tax bill on the average home in Bellflower by approximately $5.00. We don't know of any better way to spend $5.00. These youngsters of yours will be in the 1st grade, the 3rd grade, or the 5th grade but one year during their entire lives. If they must spend any one of those years in a half-day session, their educational experience will of necessity be limited. It is a loss that can never be regained. We believe we would be remiss as school administrators and that the citizens of our community would be remiss as patrons of our school unless they took every reasonable step to reduce or eliminate this vicious half-day sessioning which now is present in thirty of our classes and will, within a few years, characterize many more of them unless new buildings are made available.

Nice use of concession here

I feel sure that you people, leaders in our community, sensitive to its needs and ambitious for its improvement, will favor the bond issue which we are suggesting. But I would solicit tonight more than your passive acceptance. We would like to designate you as "The Citizens' Committee for School Housing." We would like your individual names to appear on the publicity which will be given to our community as we launch a bond-issue campaign. We would like for you to take active leadership in carrying the story of our needs to your individual organizations and to your friends and neighbors generally. We would like many of you to be a part of a Speakers Bureau which we shall organize to promote this bond campaign. In general, we would like for you to help us carry the load. Certainly the Board of Trustees or the Superintendent of Schools cannot "sell" this program alone, nor should we. No school system will be better than the community wants it to be. We believe that you people want a school system second to none. We hope that you will want to help us convince the to-

Return to pride and family love

*The final
appeal can't
miss now*

tal community that such must be the nature of our
school system. I know that you agree that our children are our most precious possessions and that their
welfare is our greatest concern. May we count on
you to help us?

2 TO EXPLAIN A PROCESS

OCCASION: Before audiences who have called you in to clarify some proposal with which you are identified. In direct sales talks and in any teaching situation.

DESIRED RESPONSE: The listener will understand the process.

METHODS: As a rule, the first step is to get an outline based strictly upon the process. In no other speech situation is success so entirely dependent upon arrangement of ideas. Allow more time for the tough spots of the process. Use clear wording and see to it that the listeners are keeping up with you.

You will very likely use visual aids in this situation. If you are using graphic materials or demonstration, remember that timing is very important. The usefulness of distributed samples or demonstration lies in proper timing. Don't send samples into the audience to compete with your spoken explanation. Don't set up a chart before a group of listeners and thereafter spend all of your time ignoring the listeners and talking to your materials. Above all, use graphic materials only with some specific and well-thought-out purpose. Such materials should aid and fortify the verbal explanation or they should be avoided.

A surprisingly large part of the public has defective vision of one kind or other; be sure that your "before the group" figures are clearly visible from all parts of the room. Lean over backwards in this respect; if in doubt make the figures bigger and bigger. Most of us have suffered through descriptive talks that employed "invisible" visual materials. This is a good place to remind you that the dirtiest trick a speaker can play on those who immediately follow on the program is to leave pictures and samples floating around in the audience.

Some Don'ts

Don't use a rambling, chatty arrangement. Don't forget the listener will be just about as interested as you are.

If using visual aids:

Don't huddle with your materials.
Don't let your samples compete with you.
Don't use graphic materials just to be using graphic materials.
Don't get in your own way while demonstrating.
Don't use materials you can't handle expertly.

The following is an example of the more-or-less informal explanation of how to do something.

How to Sell a House

You people are selling or intend to sell houses in this area. I will try to do for you what you asked me to do — give you a few hints on the steps to take before and during the setting up of a real estate sale. This on the theory that if these stages are properly handled, there will not need to be any after-sales activity.

Visiting with the audience

By now you know that we real estate folks take an awful beating among the jokesters. We are pictured selling lovely homes that turn out to be ten feet under water at high tide, of sending a crew around to take the trees down and roll up the lawn after the customer is gone, and so forth. Actually the seller gets about as much punishment as he gives in a day of activity.

General organization presented here

To get down to the business we came for, however, let's ask ourselves some questions. What do I have to sell? What are the facts on the prospect?

There are, of course, several parts to that first one. Here they are. What is the legal status of the property? Know this beyond all possibility of question. You can't, and I'm sure you wouldn't want to try to pass a bad title. I have known a few green salesmen who have sort of assumed that the owner knew his own property and had taken care of the deed. Check this right away and avoid a lot of wasted effort later. Things some people don't know about a title will floor you. You will get this legal information at the recorder's office in your court house. Check for tax status at the treasurer's office.

Now the details

Then there is the question of the condition of the property. How old is it? Is the structure sound? Good foundation, level floors, one or two stories, floor plan, plumbing, garage, storage space, closets, toilets, wiring, insulation. These are the main things to know about. A final note here, too. Look for any peculiarities. I'll never forget a friend of mine who went out to check on a property he had just listed only to find out that it had an exterior made of sea shells.

Vivid example

Now there's bound to be somebody here who is wondering what we can do about it if there are certain things wrong with a place. That depends, of course, on what's wrong. I guess all of you know, for example, that bad windows aren't hard to fix or replace, while a bad frame and floor are sometimes hopeless or so expensive you couldn't think of getting them corrected. In the same way a bad interior wall arrangement can be corrected quite economically in some homes, while in others it would break you. With all the turning to dry wall construction of late there is more that can be done in this particular kind of repair and renovation work.

Note direct reference to listeners. A good attention-getter.

Before you show anybody a place study it for such things as insulation and heating units. It doesn't inspire much confidence in a prospect to find out that the man trying to sell him a property doesn't know whether it's insulated or where, how well it's wired and whether for standard and heavy outlets. About the heating and cooling, temperature control as we call it now, well, even in the age of "pay and say nothing" there are people who want to know whether the furnace is gas or oil, and just about what the average bill has been for the heat. It seems to me in my experience that this question has often been just about decisive. It clinches or kills the sale. So be informed on fuel costs and prices.

Personal proof

Now another step to take before you take the prospect out to see the house. Get all the information you can on the site. Not just the kind of neighborhood, although goodness knows that is very important, but the width and depth of the lot, the soil and landscaping, and the improvements. A final point right here. Be ready to answer questions on street level and drainage. Be prepared to promise a dry basement under all normal conditions, or let them know just what they can expect. When you have pretty well informed yourself on the property itself, or think you have, check yourself with the questions I have just covered.

Note how a special problem is highlighted

Now you are ready to get the lowdown on the prospect. It will not only save you a lot of time in selecting sites to show him, but will enable you to get him together with the property much better, if you know his special needs, likes, and economic status. Even in this day of nothing down and a century to pay, there will be some money involved. Lack of it can be decisive, naturally. You may have the family and the "just right" home. A few thousand dollars down may keep them apart, however.

We sell a number of homes in this business to people whose families are shrinking; kids growing up, getting married, leaving home. By far the larger group of sales are made to young couples, though, and these are expanding families. These folks may be buying with the definite knowledge that the house will need to be enlarged as the family grows. A good salesman will want to check on whether he has a shrinking or an expanding family prospect. This information will help save time for both parties.

You can, of course, look over the list of needs sent in by the various potential buyers. There's this about it, however. Many a prospect will finally come out with a place that doesn't even faintly resemble the requirements he started out with. Don't hesitate, therefore, to show some borderline properties — sometimes they may hit the viewer just right even when he had no idea of such a house when he told you his needs at the start. Every year in our company, men wind up selling eight room homes to five room prospects, and vice versa. I am not suggesting that you try a lot of high pressuring on these people. It's simply that there were times when a buyer wasn't sure what he wanted until he saw it.

I like to recommend to the salesman, especially the young one, that he learn all he can about the prospect, and then that he *put himself in the buyer's place*. Represent the prospect. Be helpful in those terms. This way I think you are going to be surprised at how fast the deals can be closed, and how much fun you'll get out of getting the right thing for both parties.

Now that we know the property and the prospect pretty well, let's show the place. There are a lot of ways to do this job, naturally, so I am leaving only a few snappy rules that we use. 1. Give them time. 2. Show them the oustanding features. 3. Be ready to answer questions. 4. Make suggestions that can remove objections.

This step treated rather briefly. Does his explanation seem adequate?

Finally, gentlemen, thanks for the chance to talk here. I like real estate men. I mentioned before what a bunch of pirates we are often supposed to be. The truth is that by and large we are a good lot. I think that the very fact that a man wants to get into

141

*An inspira-
tional
touch here.
Return to
humor, also.*

this field is almost proof enough for me that he is going to be good at it. You've "got to want to," as somebody put it, if you are going to be able to sell real estate. I guess you men will do all right on that basis. At any rate, happy house hunting.

3 TO SECURE GOOD WILL

OCCASION: In a broad sense it is hard to imagine a speech situation in which one would not wish to secure good will. Cicero specifically recommended that the introduction of every speech be devoted to this purpose. Nevertheless, there are certain occasions in which securing good will is the primary purpose — before conferences, for example, or at dinners or convention assemblies where you are acting as "ambassador" or at which you are the representative of some new business or professional connection,

DESIRED RESPONSE: To make listeners feel well disposed toward you and the organization you represent. In other words good public relations.

METHODS: Look pleasant, get them to smile with you, let them know you are glad to be there. Since it is difficult to spend much time in sweet nothings, flattery of your listeners, and funny stories, perhaps the best form for such a speech to take is that of straight information. Tell them pertinent facts about your organization, highlighting characteristics which will inspire confidence and friendliness. Put your company before them in the best light.

Some Don'ts

Don't flatter too often or too openly.
Don't be unrelievedly funny.
Don't forget that in the final analysis good will is felt toward people, not companies and projects.
Don't hesitate to use the facts.

This address by Roger M. Blough, Chairman of the Board of United States Steel Corporation, delivered before The Economic Club of Chicago, March 13, 1957, is an excellent example of "good will" speaking.

GREAT EXPECTATIONS

The "glad to be here" approach used very effectively. Appeal to local pride associated with bigness.

Being in Chicago tonight is a most happy circumstance for me, because I have something on my mind which seems to fit right into this Chicago setting. We all know that Chicago has many outstanding attributes such as its beautiful lake front, its civic pride, fine suburban communities, and its great educational and cultural centers.

But to any visitor, I suppose, the one outstanding attribute which impresses him most immediately is the fact that Chicago is big — big in a lot of ways. You have a big population, big buildings, big industries, and big newspapers. You have big arteries of commerce and big markets . . . in fact, you are the center of probably the biggest market of all so far as steel products are concerned. Beyond that, you have big men with big ideas; and it is even said by some that you have a big-league pennant winner — some fine year, that is.

So the one thing that stands out on every street corner, and in every one of your actions, is bigness. That is the setting in which you live; and presumably you like it and believe in it or you wouldn't have it that way.

It is no mere happenstance, therefore, that United States Steel Corporation has located the biggest segment of its production here in the Chicago area. It is because you want big production. You like it, you believe in it — you expect it. And because you want and expect still more of it, we are engaged here today in one of the biggest programs for the expansion of existing plants that we have ever undertaken anywhere.

When that job is finished, of course, we will be even bigger than we are now. And so, perhaps, will Chicago. But according to some of you who are short of steel, we still won't be big enough!

So I think of no more appropriate setting in which to discuss the subject that is on my mind: this business of bigness . . . and vice versa — the bigness of business. But since the purely economic aspects of that issue have been debated exhaustively — though inconclusively — ever since the Twentieth Century began, I should like to attempt a more philosophical approach, based upon a proposition which seems to be axiomatic. And the proposition is this:

That the great enterprises of America are the result — simply and solely — of the great expectations of the American people. *The topic sentence.*

Despite all the frustrating lessons of history, it has always been the nature of man to harbor great expectations. And down through the ages, it has been the purpose of man to fashion for himself the instruments through which those expectations could be realized. As his expectations have increased in size and scope, so too have the industrial instruments, organizations, and agencies which he has created. And any arbitrary limitation that may be placed upon the size or scope of these instruments — either by legislative edict or tax subterfuge — must automatically place similar limits upon the realization of man's expectations. Thenceforth, and beyond those limits, his dreams would be empty and sterile.

Today, in America, we have more than four and a quarter million business units of every size and type which are designed to meet the needs and wants of our people. Many of these are very small enterprises and their number is growing as the variety of our demands increases. A few of them are very big businesses; and their size is growing as the expectations of our people soar to new and stratospheric heights.

*Nice use
of emotional
proof and
subtle
flattery.
The people
themselves
have created
the tools —
the people
must protect
them.*

But when we stop to think about it, we realize of course that the American people themselves — by their actions as consumers, investors, and workers — have created all of these instruments; and that by simply withholding their patronage, their investment, or their services, these people can regulate — or even destroy — their handiwork as their changing expectations may require.

Thus it is clear, I believe, that what an informed people think and want in this native land of ours will determine the ultimate destiny of your business and mine. And fortunately, we have an informed people — informed in more ways, through more media, and to a higher degree, than anywhere else that I know of.

So it might be profitable to examine briefly just what it is that an informed public expects of business — and especially that extra something which it is coming to expect of big business.

And quite properly, of course, the first thing that an informed people expects of any good-sized corporation is to be kept informed about its affairs.

When we go into the baker's shop on the corner, it does not occur to us to ask how much profit the proprietor is making, or how much he is paying the help in the kitchen. We merely ask the price of the product, judge the quality for ourselves, and make up our minds accordingly.

But it is quite different in the case of a big business, or of any business that is of outstanding importance to the community in which it operates. Here people do want to be informed about what wages the company is paying — whether they are too low or too high, and what effect they will have upon prices and inflation. They want to know what kind of salaries are paid to the executives — about profits and costs and dividends and competition — who owns the company, and what it produces — about all of its comings and goings. In short, they want to be able to judge for themselves whether or not the business in question is measuring up fully to their expectations of it.

And big business, of course, does provide this information to the public — not only through the records it files with governmental agencies and trade associations; but also through its detailed annual reports, proxy statements, news releases, and many other media. So big business lives and works in a goldfish bowl, where all the world can watch it — mostly because the informed expect that of big business.

Now I suppose that when you get right down to cases, the fundamental thing that people expect of business in general is to deliver the goods, so to speak. . . .

Very well put

And in this respect, too, I believe that the record will show beyond doubt that not only do the informed expect more of bigness than of business generally but that big business has measured up to the expectations of the public which created it. This is probably one of the major reasons why more people than ever before express the view that big business is a good thing for our country. In fact, 80 per cent now hold this belief, according to a recent public opinion survey. . . .

But just as the American people expect us to produce all the things they wish to buy, so they also want us to provide the wherewithal to buy them. And so — among all of their great expectations — the outstanding one, perhaps, is that business — and here again the emphasis is on big business — should play its full part in supplying enough new jobs to meet the ever-increasing requirements of our rapidly growing population.

They demand, moreover, that these shall be the better jobs, with good pay and good benefits. Yes, here, again, an informed public always seems to expect a little bit more — a plus, if you please — from big business, when it comes to good jobs.

They believe that big business is better able than small business is to devote its time, energy, and money to the development of safeguards against industrial accidents. They also believe that it should concern itself deeply with the security of its employees and their families — that it should in proper ways help these workers to insure themselves against the hazards of serious illness, old age, and lay-offs. . . .

So two of the most important things that Americans expect of industry are constantly improving production and better and better jobs. And next on their list, probably, is their insistent expectation in the field of research.

Now this expectation, of course, falls directly on the shoulders of big business. It is true that much of the individual inventive genius of our people finds its natural outlet through the small enterprises that have contributed so richly to our national progress. But small business, as a whole, has neither the manpower nor the money to support the broader programs of basic research in the fields of fundamental and applied science. Its limited resources must be devoted in the main to the manufacture and sale of its product.

Nice "We have done it because you people have demanded it" approach. Good job in public relations.

So when our people decide, for example, that they want an airborne machine that will travel many times faster than the speed of sound — and when they discover that no metal known today will withstand the terrific heat which is generated by atmospheric friction at that particular speed — they do not take their problem to the local blacksmith. They turn to United States Steel, or to one of its major competitors, to devise a brand new combination of metals that will defy the thermal barrier. . . .

And next we come to what I regard as the key to America's industrial success: competition. Over the years, I have studied the writings of many of our theorists upon this subject; and I have marvelled

at their semantic brilliance. As a steelman, moreover, I have had to cope with the practical facts of
some mighty tough competition. But I frankly con-
fess that I am still a little hesitant to try to state with
any certainty exactly what it is that an informed
public expects of big business in this area — unless it
is these things:

First, that competition from big business shall
never prevent the steady establishment and growth
of new and small business. Nor has it done so; for
the number of business units continues to grow more
rapidly than the population, and for every company
that failed last year, eleven new corporations were
established. . . .

Needed reassurance for small business and its friends.

Another important fact which is beginning to
be more widely understood, I think, is that while
some big businesses have grown bigger over the
years, industry as a whole has grown even more rapidly, so that today a single big business represents a
diminishing segment of our total economy — a
smaller proportion of the whole business community, if you see what I mean.

Thus back in 1909, U.S. Steel's assets repre-
sented 22 per cent of all of the assets of the 100
largest industrial corporations in America. But by
1955, that 22 per cent had shrunk to 4 per cent, even
though U.S. Steel's assets themselves had more than
doubled in this period. In other words, as new industries were born and other companies grew, U.S.
Steel, although itself a growth company, became
less than one-fifth as large proportionately as it was
fifty years ago.

A fairly hard statistical point made quite easy for the listener. Proportions are not easy "by ear."

By the same token, we find that at the beginning of the century, U.S. Steel produced 67 per cent
of all of the steel that was made in this country. Today it can only produce between 29 and 30 per cent,
despite the fact that its tonnage capacity has almost
quadrupled in the meanwhile.

So it is evident, I think, that big business has

not stood as any threat to the establishment and growth of smaller enterprise in this country. It is also evident, I believe, that the laws governing business competition have been effective and have measured up fully to the purpose for which they were enacted.

Now second, it seems to me that the informed expect big business to be progressive in its competition. They do not want it to become fat and lazy and complacent — clinging to old products and old models, old styles and old concepts. And if it does so, the people need no help from government in dealing with the situation. They merely put the offending company on the shelf and out of business, whatever its size may be. . . .

And third, I believe that informed people expect big business to compete realistically and in accordance with the best commercial concepts of the American market place. . . .

So in the same way, I believe, informed people expect big business to price its products with some relation to its costs and yet meet its competition in the market place. That it does try to meet its competitor's price is not, to them, a sinister indication of monopoly. Nor are they so wedded to the law of supply and demand that they expect any business — as an evidence of competition — to gouge them for all that the traffic will bear in times of shortage, or to sell at a loss in times of surplus, thus paying its customers, in effect, to carry its products away.

Well-selected examples here

They just expect vigorous, healthy, intelligent competition — theorists to the contrary, notwithstanding.

And outside the realm of competition and research and jobs and production, they expect many other things, too.

Among these, they look to big business to discharge fully its obligations as a corporate citizen of the community. Beyond the heavy burden of taxation that it bears, they expect it to contribute both time and money to civic improvement, charity drives, hospitals, schools, and recreational facilities. And when a new need arises they are very likely to look to big business first.

In this connection it is interesting to note that since the U.S. Steel Foundation was set up five years ago, the list of corporations aiding higher education has grown from a few hundred to many thousands, including more than 5,000 corporations or corporate-financed foundations which are aiding the liberal arts college groups. And the number is growing.

Still another plus which the informed expect from bigness, of course, is leadership; and I am not sure that we have always been as successful in meeting these expectations as we have been in other cases. . . .

But they have, I believe, been more successful in meeting the final expectation on the list of those that I shall discuss here tonight: and that is the responsibility of business to plan ahead, and to provide the American people with the natural resources that they must have in order to insure their industrial future.

Today our big corporations are pushing the search for iron ore, and oil and bauxite and other vital raw materials, to the farthest corners of the earth. In many industries, like steel, moreover, they are developing costly new processes for the manufacture of usable raw materials out of low-grade deposits which were once thought to be worthless. And in both of these ways, our big companies are uncovering reserves that will satisfy the needs of our nation far beyond the lifetime of any of the corporate executives who are now planning and directing the search.

Now I have covered a few of the more important things which an informed public expects of bigness in our enterprise system; and it seems to me that they raise a very interesting and challenging question. The question is: How big must business be if it is going to measure up fully to the great expectations of our people?

*Note
nice job
of pointing
up need
for more
bigness*

Well, if we look at the facts realistically, we are bound to conclude, I believe, that even some of our biggest corporations are rapidly getting too small to do all of the things that are expected of them. . . .

So it would seem that we are now witnessing another significant step in the evolution of big business. First came the individual entrepreneur; then the partnership in which a number of people pooled their resources and their managerial skills; then the modern corporation where hundreds of thousands of persons provide the necessary capital and share the risks involved; and now we see these great corporations themselves necessarily forming partnerships — for one reason and one reason alone: to do the job that is expected of them in an enterprise system where size and responsibility are companion words.

*Note
question
with no
answer.
A good
"shock"
technique.*

Does this joint development idea, perhaps, presage the birth of even larger joint ventures in business enterprise than our present-day organizations?

I wouldn't know, nor shall I even venture a prophecy.

But when I see our population doubling and, perhaps, redoubling in a single century, when I see the standard of living rising all over the world, when I contemplate the enormous drain on our natural resources in the coming century, when I witness man's first faltering steps in an atomic age, when I watch him seeking to penetrate outer space, when I see him trying to harness the rays of the sun, when I observe his determination to unlock, if he can, the ultimate secrets of the universe — such as the creation of matter out of energy — and when I comprehend, in short, the boundlessness and vastness of his expectations, I do know one thing:

That the future is not for little men with little minds. It is not for men without vision who fear progress. It is not for timid men who early were frightened by the story of Frankenstein. And it is not for those arch reactionaries who seek to shatter big enterprise and to force American industry back into the puny production patterns of its Nineteenth Century infancy.

Inspiration — challenge for the future

No. The future is for men who dare to have great expectations; and who — with the guidance and encouragement of all the people for whom they strive — will also have the courage, the persistence, the wisdom, and the patience to transform those expectations into realities!

4 TO REPORT ON A PROJECT

OCCASION: Before groups who are interested financially or personally in the project, or before listeners whose interest must be enlisted.

DESIRED RESPONSE: The securing by the listeners of the complete picture of the progress or completion of the project. The realization of the worthwhileness of the project and a desire to support it will be secondary results.

METHODS: The outline should provide a progression, although the speaker may wish to start with brief references to certain highlights. The language should be selected for exactness. The point is to tell just what you've done — no more, no less. After pre-speech audience analysis you may decide to introduce your report with a joke or a humorous remark, but before a group which is already backing you and therefore doesn't need persuading this is likely to be merely a boring preliminary.

Always leave time for questions. As a matter of fact, if the group is small enough, it may be advisable to invite interruptions for questions. If you are going to do this, however, you had better arrange to be seated throughout the report.

The key qualities of the report, whether written or oral, are completeness, exactness, and honesty. In the scientific or engineering report there should be no axe to grind. If the report doesn't present all the facts, it is a failure. The language used here should be uncolored and free from emotional loading.

Some Don'ts

Don't try the technique of revelation.
Don't be mysterious — suspense is not good here.
Don't cover up the bad results. Face your problems and explain.
Don't forget to report matters about which you know your particular listeners will want to hear.

A Report to the Building Committee
of the —— —— Church

Gentlemen, I have good and bad things to report to you as we pass the three-quarter mark in our fund-raising campaign. Whereas we have succeeded beyond our early hopes in some directions, the campaign is lagging in at least two respects. But the figures will tell you the story better than I can.

Brief enough

Good transition

In the first place let us look at the overall figures. We have total pledges amounting to $349,090. Of this sum $90,000 is available in cash. This leaves us approximately $150,000 short of our goal of $500,000 in pledged funds.

Gets right down to cases

Now, these figures do not look bad in themselves, and your fund raising committee is not too pessimistic about the prospects of reaching the half million mark by November first. It is a matter of some concern to us, however, that our team leaders report a great falling off in subscriptions in the last two weeks. This should not be interpreted as a tightening up on the part of those contacted. Unfortunately, it rather indicates that the most productive contacts have been tapped already. Let's look at the group reports, in order that we may see just how this works out.

As you know, we divided the membership to be appealed to into four groups or blocs, A, B, C, and D. The A bloc has now been rather completely

*The present
picture in
dollars and
cents*

canvassed. Note on the chart that nearly $150,000 of the present fund was raised among the members of this bloc. The B group, as you can see, has accounted for $92,000, while the D group accounts for all but $25,000 of the remainder. . . .

Our concern is centered right here. You will remember that in our preliminary projection we had worked on the assumption that group A would provide $200,000, B $150,000, and groups C and D each $75,000. With the campaign now three fourths completed the picture looks this way.

*The good
news —
and the
bad*

Group A is well up to schedule. We have had a splendid response and it seems likely that the quota here will be met with no difficulty. . . . Group B's present figure of $92,000 is less encouraging. Most of the supporters in this bloc have already pledged. Frankly we must count this total a disappointment. I should think we could safely presume that group B will not yield the projected sum of $150,000. Our team personnel found the members on the D list most cooperative — several of them oversubscribed. Unaccountably the C group, on whom we relied for a similar amount, have not been so productive. Barring the rather remote possibility that follow-ups on eleven members should be unexpectedly productive, this bloc will fall short of expectations.

To summarize, Gentlemen, we have raised to date the sum of $349,090 in pledges. Of this sum $90,000 is already available in cash. Although we have not given up all hope of reaching the goal of $500,000, we believe it is realistic to anticipate that we will fall approximately $75,000 short by our November deadline.

*A touch of
praise helps*

*The building
committee
needn't be
thanked for
listening
to this
report*

I cannot close this report without expressing my sincere admiration for all members of the canvassing teams. They have done their work exceptionally well and deserve the thanks of all of us. And remember, we are still on the job. I thank you for your attention.

5 THE INSPIRATIONAL SPEECH

OCCASION: At conventions and conferences. When you are asked to speak at gatherings designed to provide a chance for a group to get together, meet the members and talk shop. Your job is to bring inspiration for the future.

DESIRED RESPONSE: A feeling of enthusiasm, dedication, and inspiration. Increased spirit and energy for the cause should result.

METHODS: It is easy to take a cynical attitude toward the inspirational speech. Many a convention-goer has looked forward to the key speech at his convention with a combination of tolerance and amusement as something to be endured but not taken too seriously. I am afraid your author once felt the same way. Over the years I have found, however, the reason why inspirational, "pep talk," speaking continues to hold a prominent spot on convention schedules. Many people get a great deal from such talks. When intelligently prepared and sincerely presented inspirational speeches do give a real lift to the members, do send them away refreshed and rededicated to the task at hand.

As a rule this material will come in combination with some reporting on the organization's progress, or as part of the process of laying out future plans. Much political speaking is designed, not to prove anything, not to sell anything but simply to add fire to the activities of the party workers. As plans for the campaign are reported, emotional appeals are added.

As quotas are announced and the year's activities are plotted in industrial meetings, the speaker may well mix in some frankly emotional matter designed to motivate the assembled members for the job ahead.

The technique of inspirational speaking involves appeals to the broad basic drives, to loyalty and sentiment and pride. The short narrative is good here — the incident that points up the importance of wholehearted participation.

Some Don'ts

Don't act apologetic.
Don't hesitate to use sentiment.
Don't try to whip them into line.
Don't overdo the old "college spirit" angle.

The following talk delivered by Clarence J. Myers, President of the New York Life Insurance Company, at the 1953 Top Club Meetings does a good job of combining general report and inspirational follow-up.

THE SOURCES OF OUR STRENGTH

In former years at Club meetings I have reported to you on some of the Company's activities during the preceding year. And this year too I could tell you of Nylic's accomplishments, and they are considerable ones during 1952.

Statistical materials good — brief and impressive

I could tell you for example that individual life insurance sales during 1952 amounted to more than $940,000,000 and that total sales passed a billion dollars.

I could tell you that our assets have reached nearly five and one-half billion dollars.

I could tell you that New York Life is now providing protection to the owners of more than four million policies, with individual life insurance in force at nearly eleven and one-half billion dollars.

Many important achievements are a part of the record of our combined efforts in 1952. But the more I thought about my visit with you at this meeting, the more I felt there was something additional which I wanted to say. Is there not another dimension to our affairs than facts, figures, charts, graphs and records?

There is a story they tell on one of the islands of the South Pacific about the origin of Man. According to this ancient tale, two things were given to Man to set him apart from the other creatures of the earth. The first was the gift of hands, so articulated that Man could grasp objects with his fingers and thumbs. The second was the gift of imagination.

Used story as point of departure for self-analysis

With his hands, Man fashioned many things for his desire, his comfort and his convenience. With his hands he assembled the material resources which gave physical shape and dimension to his life and a measure of material security for his future. And these things he did alone.

The second gift, imagination — an intangible thing — transformed Man's intelligence. It lifted him out of his circumscribed and literal life. With it, he imagined a better shelter for his family, and he became a builder. He imagined himself better armed and a great hunter, and he became a great hunter.

But Man soon found that his imagination also created within him new fears. Alone, his weaknesses and fears were very real to him, and he almost regretted the gifts he had received. Then his imagination told him he could get along better in this strange, wonderful world if he were part of something larger than himself.

In this way, he felt he would not only be safer, but he would also be provided with an intangible source of strength and inspiration. And so Man joined with other men for their common welfare, and together they created institutions to serve their needs.

I like this story from the other side of the world. And by extension I believe it has meaning for all of us.

In our busy, encumbered lives, it is difficult to take perspective upon ourselves. We are apt to become so preoccupied with the multitude of benefits at our fingertips that we become careless of how and why they came to us. How are we sustained? What are the sources of our strength?

If we stop to think about this for a moment, I believe one thing will become more and more clear to us — something we all realize, I suppose, but are inclined to forget. Is it not true, though many centuries have passed since that story was first told in the South Pacific, we are no different today in certain essential respects from that early Man in the dawn of human history? For like him, we too draw our strength and inspiration from something outside of ourselves and bigger than ourselves. From our religious faith. From our love of our homes and families. From our ideal of free government. From our great institutions.

Inspirational materials here based on reporting of company accomplishment

You may not have thought of a business enterprise as a great institution. And of course all business enterprises are not great institutions. They become so only through the nature of their purpose and performance. They become so when they serve human needs and when their conduct is on the highest level of morality.

Through noble purpose and responsible performance, a business enterprise becomes more than a business enterprise. It becomes an institution. And when it does these things greatly, it becomes a great institution. And like New York Life it remains a great institution because its people have an abiding sense of its greatness. . . .

Now I want to say something about the business enterprise, New York Life, with which all of us here have so intimately identified ourselves.

I am reporting to you that it is a great and strong institution. It is a vital institution. I know that it is a source of inspiration for you and for me.

Throughout the history of our Company men and women have striven to keep these convictions fresh and alive. Their labor endows our present efforts with deeper meaning, as it emboldens our vision.

Return to reporting here

The nature of New York Life's strength is difficult to define precisely because much of it is so intimately involved with the human spirit which defies definition. Are we strong and vital because we are materially strong? Of course. There is no need to tell you that no life insurance company enjoys a stronger position than ours.

But material resources alone do not explain our strength. Material resources are important, as hands are important. But we know, you and I, that there is something more. There is something intangible which articulates these hands. We can suggest what it is, but because it is largely composed of intangibles we cannot give it a name which will identify the whole.

Is it the skill and experience we possess? Yes, of this I am sure. It is in recognition and in honor of your skill and experience as individuals that we are gathered here today.

Is it moral courage? A deep and abiding sense of responsibility? Is it strength of purpose? Yes, I am sure it is all of these things. But such words as these are inadequate symbols when we try to put them to work to explain the intangible. How then can we know the nature of our institution, that vital source we call New York Life?

When I reach for the answer there comes to my mind a random variety of pictures and incidents.

There comes to my mind a frail, old lady of 97 who is known around Independence County, Arkansas, as Aunt Mary. She had never seen an electric light until last August 28. On that day a new line of the Arkansas Power and Light Company

Use of numerous pertinent cases

reached her home. New York Life had a share in this historic moment for Aunt Mary, because our investment in the power company helped to make it all possible.

There comes to my mind a magazine article by Lewis Mumford, the celebrated architectural critic. After a visit to New York Life's residential development Fresh Meadows on Long Island, Mr. Mumford said, "Great is a word I use sparingly, especially about housing projects, but when I first saw the plans for Fresh Meadows, I had a hunch that this was the word. Fresh Meadows is perhaps the most positive and exhilarating example of large-scale community planning in this country."

There come to my mind the 400 members of our Nylic Home Office staff who are devoting their time and energies to learning through weekly conference discussions in our management development program how to become better managers of our Company's operations. . . .

Appeals to pride

There come to mind the two New York Life agents, now Marine Corps jet pilots, who have completed 121 missions between them over Communist-held North Korea.

There come to my mind the 31 educational programs conducted at the Home Office to teach our people at all levels how to do more things at less cost.

There come to my mind the many talented men and women who are at work to keep our Company vital and progressive. For example there is the Home Office committee which is studying the application of electronic machines to our staggering problem of record-keeping. . . .

There comes to my mind a letter we received at the Home Office last winter. It is reprinted in this year's annual report to policyholders. Perhaps you have had an opportunity to read it and were touched as I was when you read it. You will recall that it was from a young woman in Butte, Montana, whose husband was killed last year in a tragic mine accident. To me it is one of the finest tributes to the Agency people of our Company I have ever seen.

In her letter, the young woman, a widow with a small child, said, "I am very proud of our association with the New York Life Insurance Company, and immensely grateful to a company which has on its staff of agents such a man as John Kosena. His reputation in Butte is an enviable one, as hosts of friends and neighbors will prove. It is a wonderful thing to know that his able hand is guiding my own future and that of innumerable policyholders to whom he has sold insurance. This letter, then, is my thank-you for making it possible for me to face a future which could have been terribly dark and uncertain had it not been for John Kosena, who is certainly one of the 'good men to know.' "

How can we know the nature of our institution?

Matthew said, "By their fruits ye shall know them." We of the New York Life are known by our deeds which speak with greater eloquence than words or numbers. We realize, as someone has said, that conduct is three-fourths of life and its largest concern. As a company we are rich in years; but years alone count for little unless we are also rich in deeds.

I am proud to tell you that the great institution, New York Life, to which we dedicate so many hours of our days, has the compass, the vigor and the vision to serve mankind well. For along with our great sources of strength and inspiration it, too, is a vibrant source of strength and inspiration for each of us who wants it to be.

Let me repeat: for each of us who wants it to be. If we just don't care — if it doesn't mean much to us that we are life insurance people with a hundred reasons to be excited by the challenges and opportunities in our work — if it doesn't mean much to us that we represent New York Life with a thousand reasons to be proud of its great traditions, its great reputation, its high place in the business — if we are not stirred, in our minds and hearts, by our calling and by our Company, then these words of mine will be meaningless. For this great institution of ours will not strengthen and inspire those who look to it unthinkingly and unfeelingly. One takes from it as one gives.

A challenge for the future after the picture of a satisfactory present

If we are to keep the New York Life the living entity it is, if we are to keep vital this inherited idea which is animated by the hopes and needs of human beings everywhere, we must know in our hearts that each of us is a part of this living entity. I believe — I deeply believe — that as we know this in our hearts, and as we strive to keep this ideal alive so it will sustain and strengthen us beyond our greatest expectations. And from it we shall draw new vision and vigor and power — each of us — to bring to the day's work; and we shall know a deeper contentment because of what we have achieved . . . yes, and because of what we have set for ourselves to achieve tomorrow.

We are the keepers, you and I, of the vital sources of our Company's strength. It is a precious, historic trust. By our actions we keep that trust.

6 TO SPEAK IN PRAISE

OCCASION: At political gatherings, testimonial dinners, or any place where someone is being honored. Much of this sort of thing occurs in the introduction of speakers by the chairman on formal occasions.

DESIRED RESPONSE: The audience will be brought to a greater realization of the virtue and ability of the man honored, while the subject of the praise will, of course, be gratified unless the occasion is posthumous.

METHODS: Draw upon all that you know about the subject and all that those in the best position to know can tell you of his virtues and accomplishments. If anything has been printed about him read that. Once you have this material it is to be hoped that it adds up to adequate evidence of praiseworthiness. In any event remember that on occasions for praise the speaker may safely go "all out" for his subject. He is not expected to stick to a bare recital of the record; rather he may well expand upon the facts to a degree ordinarily not reached in everyday speaking. Of course this doesn't mean that the praise becomes so fulsome and the phrases so lyrical that admiration is changed to suspicion. Your own good taste will be your only guide here, but it is safe to say that we no longer go in for the old eulogies that wrote their heroes indelibly upon the firmament of heaven, and sent their names ringing endlessly down the corridors of time. Use a little restraint in the modern testimonial address.

A word about your obligation to mention, amid all the sterling qualities and deeds, a few weaknesses and a failure or two. I would strongly recommend that this form of concessive technique be used very sparingly if at all in a speech of this kind.

The narrative form can be used to good advantage in this speech. Episodes from the life of your subject are most effective in pointing up certain of his admirable qualities.

The eulogy is a good place for passages from literature if you can find fresh ones.

Finally, no man was ever raised to greatness by words spoken on his behalf. The best that praise can do is to gain greater appreciation and fuller realization of the worth of the subject.

Some Dont's

Don't try to substitute flowery language for plain truth.
Don't ignore the value of formal style.
Don't minimize your man; give him full value.
Don't undertake to praise a man who doesn't deserve praise.

The following oration, delivered in 1951 by Doris Schwinn Taylor (of Southern Illinois University), is a fine example of effective speaking in praise.

SOMETHING OF A MAN

Nice use of narrative opening

A young man trudges wearily down a slag road. It is a spring afternoon in 1896. But there is no beauty here. For he walks among the miserable shacks where miners' families live, and he knows that — they are owned by the company. The food the family eats comes from a store — owned by the company. The stinking air of soot and coal dust he breathes — is owned by the company. The miner's children condemned by family need of food, enter the mines and they too are — owned by the company. The miners bury their dead, and the companies bury their living in a present and future as black as the coal pits below.

But this story is not new to this young man. He has known the desperation of hunger. His father helped lead a strike to improve hazardous conditions in a mine. The strike was won, but his father was blacklisted and forced to become a wandering exile. Only now, seventeen years later, the blacklist is destroyed.

This youth knows the future he faces. He knows the mines are dungeons without ventilation or lights where men sweat it out from ten to twelve hours a day in the suffocation of powder fumes.

In a Wyoming mine he knew human anguish and horror as cursing and shocked he helped carry out the torn bodies of 236 miners killed in an explosion. The descent into that mine was a descent into hell, but what ripped his emotions was the sight of the numb, mute faces of the wives, now suddenly widows of the men they loved. Here he was baptized in his own tears to his life-time fight for the miners.

Strong emotional appeals

The past fifty years have seen a drastic change in this young man. You would know him for his bull-dog chin, his bushy eyebrows, his unyielding stubbornness in his fight for his men. The man of whom I speak is, of course, John L. Lewis, President of the United Mine Workers of America.

And I speak because I come from a miner's home, a mining community. My father has been a miner for 42 years. Lewis has led him, with 400,000 other miners, to a new era of living. If it were not for Lewis, I would not be here; prior to the U.M.W.A., miner's children didn't attend college. Few even went to high school because money wasn't available for such frivolities.

Personal proof

Let's look at John L. Lewis for what he is to you and for what he means to me. To many of you he is a thug, a saboteur, a dictator, a man crazed with a lust for power. The press has blamed Lewis for every strike, played up his defiance of the government. I understand your attitude; and if Lewis were alone in your condemnation, I would not be overly concerned, for at times we are all misunderstood; but, he is a symbol — a symbol of the

Concession — what people hold against him

U.M.W.A. — a symbol of 400,000 miners. As you distrust Lewis, you also distrust the miners.

What are they like, these creatures who toil in dark, musty, underground caverns?

Frankly, the miner is filled with a bitterness bordering on hatred for the outside world. Its newspapers attack him, its politicians intrigue against him, his union, and his leader, John L. Lewis. The miner says, "People seem to think we are some kind of animals — underground rats." Or, "The way people outside think of us, we should be living in a zoo." One miner adds bitterly, "We'd be better fed and be a hell of a lot safer in cages!"

While America's cities still sleep, the men who mine coal are awake, moving quietly about the house trying not to disturb their sleeping children. They wash and dress by instinct in the darkness and then blink in the sudden dim light in the kitchen. There the miner's wife stands by as her husband wolfs down a massive breakfast that would be amazing to the fifty-seven per cent of Americans who live in our cities and greet the new day with the polite morning ceremonial of toast and coffee. As the sleeping city dweller stirs restlessly at 6:30, the miner has already checked in at the entrance of the mine. Then just as the sun comes up, he goes plummeting down in an elevator cage — deep into the bowels of earth.

Dramatizes the problem to be solved

The day is spent, many times, in ankle deep water. The men are surrounded by darkness so black they can feel it. It is a darkness dripping with the oily black slime of the guts of the earth. But the miner is never alone, for death is all about him. It is over his head with the collapsing roof and his sudden crushing burial; it is in front of him in the pockets of invisible, odorless, tasteless, deadly methane gas released by cutting into the coal face and ignited by his explosives. It is behind him in the long tunnels, where it comes with the reptilian hiss of the rolling wall of smoke and flame as he shakes and screams in agony knowing that death is coming either by cremation or asphyxiation.

Every day he shoots dice with death. He can verify the figures of the National Safety Council for 1949, which show that mine accidents are four times as frequent and six times as severe as the average of all industries.

He knew some of the 68,000 miners killed from 1919–45, and he knew many of the 2,275,000 injured. He has stood awkward and choked with emotion before some of the 211,000 widows and orphans of these men. He contributed to collections for the impoverished survivors with a generosity born of a deep premonition that the next collection might be for his own widow and children.

And the dead were not just those entombed below or brought up as blackened, lifeless husks inside a roll of blanket. They were next door, where as long as he could remember that miner with the broken back had been decaying in his bed inside a rotting shack. Across the road, another, paralyzed from the hips down since the blast four years ago.

Why should we be concerned with these men and their defiant leader? Simply because coal is the prime mover of our life. In these black chunks is the energy of our vast industrial empire. Coal is man's creative trinity of light, heat, and power. Half of American homes are heated by coal. Nearly 95 per cent of our railroad locomotives are driven by the fiery energy of coal. Coal is essential in the mass production of steel. The mines are an inexhaustible warehouse to our chemical industry. Coal is the base for that life-saving miracle of modern times, the sulfa drugs. From nylon to plastics, from aspirin to perfume, the list of products is as great as our coal supply; and in America, we have enough coal to last twenty-five hundred years.

What have the miners gained in their long

fight? Even since 1940, miner's hourly pay has nearly doubled; and new measures such as an hour of travel time, $100.00 vacation pay, 8½ cents lunch time pay, and fifty million dollars a year welfare fund have been added. In addition, state compensation is now compulsory, federal safety rules are enforced, the company and not the miner supplies the tools. Remember the miners' shacks as Lewis saw them fifty years ago? The home I live in might be described as a typical miner's home — a modest, six room, white bungalow, modern and comfortable. I am one of five children, and we have all had the opportunity to attend high school and later college.

I would like you to remember two things about the miner's present situation: he is finally being well paid because his is a most dangerous occupation; and, mining, in these days of coal cutters, loaders, drills, and explosives, is skilled labor comparable to any other technical field. The government knows this, and threats to have the army man the mines never were enforced. A novice couldn't mine a ton a day, compared to the regular fifteen tons per miner.

Lewis has fought this unceasing battle not only against the mine operators. The owners easily enlisted the sympathies of the press and the public, for publishers are employers with their own labor problems and a management point of view. Because the public was easily led to blame the miners for every stoppage of vital coal, Lewis has had to fight the public, too. A mine may be a death trap, working conditions and living conditions beyond human endurance; but if the miner strikes, it is he, not the owner of the mine, who is to blame in your eyes.

You may feel that Lewis's fight is justified, but that his methods are unnecessarily rough, that public hardship and expense should not be involved in a fight between operators and miners. Let me tell you from experience, the miner doesn't want to strike. A mining town during a strike is dead; potatoes and beans on credit, clothes, shoes falling apart, youngsters out of school, lights and water cut off, and it takes forever for the hard won increase to pay back for lost time. But so far the strike is their only bargaining tool. If you could come up with an effective answer, the miner would be the first to agree to do away with the strike as a means for settling disputes.

I know well this tragic story of the miner. I remember some eight years ago on my mother's birthday when we were called to come to the hospital. Daddy had a unique birthday gift for mother —. His index and middle fingers had been ground off in a cutting machine. My father was lucky; he's still alive.

More of the personal identification

Last week I heard a miner make the statement, "I've been in the mines thirty-seven years and the welfare fund makes all I have been through worthwhile." I can understand this. My father, like thousands of other miners, is suffering from miner's asthma — a condition described as a hardening of the lungs due to a layer of coal dust — a creeping death forced by the lack of oxygen. Two months ago he returned from Philadelphia, where he had been hospitalized and treated at union expense. The doctors feel they can offer him relief if not a cure from his misery of coughing and strangling for air. He can retire, thanks to Lewis's Miner's Welfare Fund.

Do you understand why I feel I owe this man a debt of gratitude? As surely as Lincoln freed the slaves, Lewis has freed the miner from a life owned by a company, from the shackles of filth and corruption, from the desperation of entering the mines without safety precautions. Actually Lewis is a symbol of America, of democracy, of what we are fighting for today in Korea — the inalienable right to be free men. Be gentle with your criticism of this man and the men he leads, for they are truly representative of the American way of life. They are the base of America's towering industrial pyramid.

John L. Lewis's death will be sadly mourned by labor. It will be cheered by operators and owners. But it is undeniable that Lewis has led this nation to an era of better living. His defiance of even the government is dramatic proof of the right of an individual or a group to fight for its security in our democracy. Will you see him with me as a courageous fighter for human rights and agree with the United Mine Workers that "he is something of a man"?

7 TO MOVE AN

AGREEABLE AUDIENCE TO ACTION

OCCASION: This is a special situation which may develop in any of the speeches which have gone before or which are likely to follow. The audience is favorably disposed toward your proposal but has not been brought to the point of doing anything about it. Your listener knows that the Community Chest is a wonderful thing, says many nice things about it, but just doesn't get around to contributing.

DESIRED RESPONSE: To get the listener to sign on the dotted line, join up, make a contribution, or go out and do something.

METHODS: If you have been having trouble pushing your listeners beyond the "amen" or "that's right" stage, you will recognize this as one of the toughest speech situations. It may best be met by appealing to some one of the basic drives. This may be fear, love, hate, greed, or pride. The speaker may minimize the value of belief without action (faith without works is dead), he may use the tomorrow-may-be-too-late angle, he may stress the point that only cowards fail to do what they know ought to be done, he may remind his listener that the man next door has already done something about it.

Some Don'ts

Don't spend much time on logical-factual proof — on that this listener is way ahead of you.

Don't go on too long. Remember Mark Twain's story of the speaker who talked his listeners into and out of the mood.

Don't stop short of action. Assign the jobs, hand out the contract, get a handshake on it, turn them loose to do it now.

Following are some examples of speech to make doers out of believers.

This puts them to work

I know that no one here believes in running the risk of depriving our children of adequate education. That's fine. That's as it should be. But you people know as well as I do that that isn't enough. Now I am going to ask every one in this audience who is willing to spend two hours this week on the job of getting people out to vote on the school bond issue to raise his hand. Why? Because every other citizen of this district is just as anxious to do right by our youth as we are, but many of them won't get around to it unless reminded. On Wednesday next we want to be very sure that our belief in education is down in black and white where it can do some good. I am going to send a man to each row in the hall with a sheet of paper. Sign your name and indicate the hours when you can help.

The rough treatment

You people have said a hundred times that you have been shocked and embarrassed by the discrimination against Negroes in our community. You've been talking this way for years. The trouble is you can go on disapproving for the next hundred years and nothing will come of it. Now if you mean what you say, if you want to put your money where your mouth is, if you want to make what you think add up to something, if you really believe what you say, join us in this campaign to secure decent treatment for an eighth of our citizens in local restaurants.

A touch of fear and affection

If, as you say, you are a great believer in life insurance; and if, as I'm sure is the case, you want to be certain that your family will be cared for in case of your death, that's all very fine. The trouble is, none of this will do your loved ones a bit of good. You can go on thinking it's a good idea for years, or weeks, or maybe days, but it won't make a bit of difference to anybody, until you take out adequate insurance.

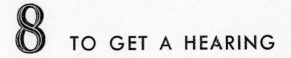

8 TO GET A HEARING

FROM A HOSTILE AUDIENCE

OCCASION: Before an audience that doesn't like you, doesn't like what you have to say, or doesn't like either you or your subject.

DESIRED RESPONSE: Willingness on the part of listeners to give you a hearing, despite an originally hostile attitude.

METHODS: All that has been said about the necessity for seeming well disposed toward your audience, well informed, and a person of good character will naturally apply in the effort to win favor with an antagonistic audience. The first step, of course, will be unusually thorough audience analysis. Such analysis will provide you with the background or the history of the hostile feeling, and when you know why the listeners are angry or reluctant, you can better do something about it. Four general methods used separately or in combination will help you get a good hearing: (1) absolute frankness; (2) mood of agreement; (3) concession, and (4) appeal to fair play.

The first of these, the method of absolute candor, is perhaps not used often enough by speakers. In many cases the suspicious listeners are completely disarmed when the speaker simply puts all his cards on the table or throws himself "on the mercy of the court," as it were. Since much hostility is based upon misunderstanding or ignorance of the other man's position, this approach is usually well worth trying.

The second method, the mood of agreement, is a matter of conditioned response. The speaker begins his speech and continues it for some time with a number of opinions and proposals to which he knows the audience is bound to answer "yes." Thus he puts the audience in an affirmative state of mind so that when he finally comes to the disputed point the listeners are in the mood to agree. When this is not handled too obviously it may be extremely effective, since the man who *feels* like saying "yes" is much more likely to say it.

The third approach which you might try is the method of concession. The speaker thinks of nice things to say about the opinion and position of the hostile listeners. This will enhance his status with the group. They are likely to think that it takes a big man to see and recognize the virtues of the other side and they are inclined to reciprocate in their attitude.

The fourth approach is the appeal to fair play. Whether or not the spirit of fair play characterizes the American public, we insist that it does, and if a speaker simply assumes audibly that his audience will give him a hearing because American people believe in fair play, he is likely to get it.

Another approach is sometimes recommended, although it is doubtful whether it is very often useful. This is the device of making your position logically inescapable. The speaker says to himself, "It doesn't matter whether they like me or like what I am telling them; if I can make it perfectly clear that I am right, good sense will make them go along with me." This approach is always risky in that most attempts to use it serve only to put the audience more on the defensive than ever. Trite though it may be to say it, a man convinced against his will is very likely to be of the same opinion still.

Some Don'ts

Don't carry a chip on your shoulder.
Don't cringe and plead for favor.
Don't allow yourself to seem worried and nervous.
Don't try to ignore hostility.

The following are examples of conciliatory speaking.

Absolute frankness with appeal to fair play

I know that you people are solidly against the new plan for districting. You have made your position pretty clear on that. Some of my friends in the west end have been telling me I was a fool to come over here and try to talk the proposal over with you. Personally I don't feel that way about it. I know how you stand and I admire you for it. I also know that you folks are fairminded citizens; your reputation for fairness is such that I didn't have the slightest hesitation in coming before you tonight.

It seems to me, gentlemen, that some people are confusing their detestation of the crime with their proper attitude toward my client. I know that you will go all the way in support of justice. I am therefore unworried. It will not escape the attention of a group of free men and citizens that a man is innocent until proved guilty. The prosecution will not sway you gentlemen with his cries against the crime; he must prove that my client is guilty of such a crime if he hopes to make any headway with this jury.

Mood of agreement with a touch of flattery

People are funny; there's no doubt about that. People are fair, too; there's even less doubt about that. They want to see the right thing done. That's why we didn't hesitate for a moment to submit our request for funds to bring needy persons from Germany over here. We know you folks will want to give these people a break they can't get without your aid.

Fair play

Five years ago this club oversubscribed for the charity fund, four years ago it raised two thousand dollars for the all-church drive, last summer it carried across the park equipment campaign almost single-handed. I know I can ignore certain whisperings I have heard about how you gentlemen are reluctant to back the Baseball for the Kids program this summer. I know you men have been called on often — no doubt more often than you should have been, but I am sure you'll help again just as I'm sure the cause is a good one.

Concession neatly employed here

Fair
play

Several people warned me about trying to speak here tonight. They told me that you folks were all Democrats and wouldn't listen to a Republican. I told them I knew you people had a Democratic voting record, but that you also had a record for fair play. "They'll give me a hearing if I lay all my cards on the table," I said, and, ladies and gentlemen, I'll bet you will.

TO PRESIDE OVER A
MEETING OF AN ORGANIZED GROUP

OCCASION: The meeting of a group of people who make up an organization and function under rules of order.

DESIRED RESPONSE: To provide for the effective conduct of business.

METHODS: The chairman of an organized meeting is in a position of peculiar responsibility in a democratic society. Upon his fairness and competence, in a real sense, will depend the effective functioning of our way of life. A fine organization with a lucid set of rules and a clear-cut constitution, will still be fumbling and ineffective if the presiding officer fails. Specifically, just what are the functions of the presiding officer?

First, he should call the meeting to order.

Second, he should call for the various reports and announcements which make up the order of the day.

Third, once debate is under way he should recognize speakers firmly and clearly.

Fourth, he should enforce the rules of the group.

Fifth, in an overall way the chairman has another duty — to set the tone and spirit of the meeting.

Obviously, the chairman must be acquainted with the special rules of his organization and with the generally accepted principles of parliamentary procedure. The final word in rules is undoubtedly Roberts' *Rules of Order*, but there are several other more concise and more easily interpreted books on the subject. Undoubtedly the main confusion in the conduct of a business meeting comes from failure to observe the precedence of motions. The following by no means complete chart will prove useful:

ORDER OF PRECEDENCE OF MOTIONS

The ordinary motions rank as follows, the lowest in rank being at the bottom and the highest at the top of the list.

Undebatable	Fix the Time to which to Adjourn (when privileged).† Adjourn (when privileged).† Take a Recess (when privileged).† Raise a Question of Privilege. Call for the Orders of the Day.	Privileged
Debatable	Lay on the Table. Previous Question. ($\frac{2}{3}$) Limit or Extend Limits of Debate. ($\frac{2}{3}$) * Postpone to a Certain Time.* Commit or refer.* Amend.* Postpone indefinitely. A main motion.*	Subsidiary

† The first three motions are not always privileged.
* Can be amended: the others cannot be amended.

To fix the time to which to adjourn is privileged only when made while another question is pending and in an assembly that has made no provision for another meeting on the same or the next day. To ADJOURN loses its privileged character and is a main motion if in any way qualified, if its effect, if adopted, is to dissolve the assembly without any provision for its meeting again. To take a RECESS is privileged only when made while other business is pending.

The necessity for fairness on the part of the presiding officer has already been mentioned. This involves scrupulous adherence to rules even when the members are perhaps not aware of the rules. It means that when two people ask for the floor at the same time the chairman will be governed by the following two things in deciding whom to recognize: whether or not one of the speakers has had the floor before, or if both have had it, who has had it more recently?

Some Don'ts

Don't take part in debate.
Don't play favorites.
Don't permit anarchy.   (Call them to order without hesitation.)
Don't use your office to railroad your pet projects.

10 TO TAKE PART

IN DISCUSSION OR CONFERENCE

OCCASION: When two or more people get together in a face-to-face situation, to arrive at a consensus as to truth, value, or proper policy in regard to some question.

DESIRED RESPONSE: Arriving at the facts, making the right judgment, settling upon the best policy, or exploring a problem.

METHODS: A leader should be appointed. He will guide the discussion, recognizing speakers and summarizing progress from time to time. Each member will enter the discussion when he has a point to make or a question to ask. Have your ideas clearly thought out before you take the floor. You may strongly urge a line of action but be ready to listen to other proposals. People being what they are, it is essential that the discussant remind himself repeatedly to give all suggestions calm and objective consideration. The group should select a clerk or secretary who will keep a record. At the end of a meeting the consensus may be put in the form of resolutions or statements of policy.

The foregoing, of course, assumes that the discussion group is being organized solely for the purpose of discussion. The suggestions will apply just as well to committee meetings, policy conferences, and "councils of war."

Some Don'ts

Don't be belligerent.
Don't hold the floor when you are not contributing.
Don't just come along for the ride; take part.

Don't advocate too strongly.
Don't monopolize the discussion.
Don't be a "yes" man — or a "no" man either.
Don't try to "hide your ignorance" in discussion.

Sample Outline for Discussion on a Question of Policy

"WHAT SHOULD BE THE ROLE OF THE UNITED STATES IN THE MIDDLE EAST?"

Session I. Definition and Limitation of the Problem

    A. What countries are included in the Middle East?
    B. What do we mean by "role"?
        1. Is it possible that we play several roles?
        2. What are some of these?
    C. What are the relationships that dictate our actions in the Middle East?
        1. As one of the two great powers?
        2. As a member of the U.N.?
        3. As a member of N.A.T.O.?
    D. What are the problems in the Middle East?
        1. Which are the countries involved in each?
        2. How does each affect us?
    E. Can all Middle East problems be confined to that area?

Session II. Analysis and Selection of Criteria

    A. What is the general historic background of the Middle East?
    B. What forces call for a change in our Middle East policy?
        1. Our rise to world leadership?
        2. The behavior of Russia in the Middle East?
        3. The special problem of Israel?
        4. American oil interests in the Middle East?
        5. Our ties with Western colonial powers?
    C. What criteria should be applied in choosing a solution?
        1. Religious?
        2. Economic?
        3. Political?
        4. Military?

Session III. Suggested Solutions

    A. Should we try the "balance of power" approach?
    B. Should we work strictly within the U.N.?
    C. Should we be influenced by self-interest?
    D. Should we put the major emphasis on world betterment?

In conferences where there is an honest desire to arrive at policy decisions the foregoing outline of procedure is good. It begins where all problem-solving must begin — with an understanding of the nature and limitation of the problem. Once agreement is reached on these points, the next step is bound to be analysis. The group will

The Saturday Evening Post

"I DON'T LIKE THE WAY HE DOMINATES THESE DISCUSSIONS!"

184

look into the causal aspects of the question. What produced the question? Why is this a problem? A history of the background of the matter under consideration belongs here. Once the members are fully informed upon the details of the problem the next step entails the selection of criteria. In other words, what are the essential features of any solution that is to be effective? What are the requirements of any policy that is to be a good one in this situation? Next comes the consideration of various suggested policies or solutions. As a final step a solution is agreed upon by the group.

In any meeting where the membership is sincere, open-minded, and genuinely interested in getting things done these so-called "reflective steps" will get results.

Beware of the so-called discussions called merely to sweeten dictatorial announcements, or to come out with certain foregone conclusions under the guise of group action. Make sure you yourself aren't guilty of axe-grinding.

If you are a leader in discussion do not try to dominate or force progress. Avoid stepping in except to summarize and suggest new areas. The best leader in reflective consideration of problems is often the one who can make his presence felt with very little noticeable participation.

Examine the following extract from a discussion on a community issue.

CHAIRMAN: We have called this meeting tonight to hear an explanation of the new proposal for a swimming pool for our community. I need not tell you people that this town feels strongly the need for such a pool. Our young people have no outdoor swimming facilities at all, and are forced to take to the streams and ponds in the neighborhood. Mr. B_____ has come here to present the proposal of the Pool Committee for raising the funds that would bring us up to modern requirements in this community, and get our kids the pool they deserve.

The chairman shouldn't take sides. He doesn't conceal his leaning adequately, it would seem. It's hard to moderate differences when you've already taken sides.

MR. B_____: Most of us agree that our young people deserve one. We are the only city of

Nice approach through the past. This confronts the group squarely with a present problem.

our size in a hundred mile radius without one. For the past three years our committee has been working hard to bring our city up to date on this matter. During that period we have petitioned twice for funds. We have attempted vainly to raise money by solicitation. Some of our citizens have responded nobly but I think it's pretty clear that we can't get the needed funds that way.

MRS. W——: Just how much money do you estimate it will take for such a pool, Mr. B——? It seems to me that I've heard something about $200,000. That seems like an unreasonable sum to be spent on mere pleasure. Now . . . .

Don't go off half-cocked. This protest is useless unless accurately documented. It's right to ask "from ignorance" — it's wrong to complain.

MR. B——: Now Mrs. W——, let me explain my plan for what you call "mere pleasure." I think as I get along with the details you'll see that the amount we ask isn't unreasonable. Some might call it unreasonably low.

MR. D——: I don't think any of the tax payers here are going to worry about how low it is. We've been taxed to death . . . .

MR. B——: Not on a pool, you haven't been taxed to death. You've not been taxed at all.

MR. D——: Yes, but we've been canvassed to death, and funded to pieces.

Temper! Mr. B——, granting the provocation, will get nowhere this way. Notice how he does better later on. Don't be a mother hen about your ideas.

Mrs. W—— is personalizing everything. We must all fight against this tendency if we are to add anything to discussion.

MRS. W——: I can say "Amen" to that. It seems to me now that every time I go to the door . . . .

Chairman breaks in nicely right here

CHAIRMAN: Friends, let's allow the committee and Mr. B—— to get their proposal before us in its entirety before we start on it.

MR. B____: Thank you, Bill. Now, we are agreed in the committee that the pool will take $150,000. That money we propose to raise by an assessment over a period of 10 years, to be discontinued when the cost of the pool has been met. This isn't a lot of money. We estimate that won't add up to much above $20.00 per tax payer in the ten-year period. Obviously this isn't going to add up to a very heavy burden on any citizen. It seems to us a very reasonable price to pay for such civic improvement. For this money we figure we can take care of our young people and move our community forward to a place it deserves in the area.

The use of figures and procedures is adequate here

This bit of advocacy seems uncalled for

MR. L____: I'd like to say that I heartily agree with B____ and his committee. The proposal is sound, inexpensive and I intend to back it. I think . . . .

MR. D____: Well maybe it seems reasonable to you but there are plenty of us who aren't going to go for any more drain on our money. It's twenty dollars now but the do-gooders around here will think of fifty other uses for our money before the ten years are up. We've got to draw the line somewhere and this is the place.

Perhaps taxes should be added to those other "topics it's useless to discuss," religion and politics. Mr. D____ has undoubtedly been badly harassed just as he says, but it's unreflective to overstress it.

MRS. W____: After all, do our kids need a pool to loaf around in all summer? What's wrong with our town now? I like it well enough. A lot of us do. It seemed like a fine place to live for years. Why put ourselves in financial straits anyway for a bunch of young juvenile delinquents who won't give you any thanks for it?

Temper again. Chances are she doesn't really mean all this.

MR. N____: Oh I don't think our kids are bad and personally I think most of us would like to see them have a pool. But there are some other questions on my mind. Where will you locate the pool, Will?

The peacemaker role well played here. Mr. N____ is a useful man to have around in a discussion.

Mr. B____: Let me answer that. It'll be on the land at the foot of Hill Park between Lake and Chestnut Streets. This land can be had at a small figure. Indeed being able to get this area is one reason why we can figure our cost so low.

Mr. D____: Low! Well, heaven help us if it had been higher.

Now D____ has earned his right to be ignored in serious discussion.

Mr. N____: Another question, folks. What arrangement does this proposal make for maintaining and staffing the pool once it's completed? I know that can be handled not too expensively but it *is* a problem that will have to be solved.

Questions help discussion. It's no disgrace not to know. The disgrace lies in remaining ignorant.

Mrs. W____: Just another cost. Maybe another assessment next year and the next. By the way tell me this. What assurance do we have that when this ten-year stretch is ended that it won't just keep on going indefinitely? We've seen that happen before in this city.

Mr. B____: Just when did this happen before, Mrs. W____?

Mrs. W____: Well, I can't come right out with a specific case but I'm sure if I had time . . . .

An obstructionist on the scent. Note what he does with a question, originally asked very objectively.

Mr. D____: The point is this. We have a good question here from Mr. N____. Where are you going to get the funds to pay for the upkeep of this swimming place?

Mr. C____: There seems to me a tendency here to cross our bridges before we come to them, doesn't there? We can raise maintenance funds each year by staging an annual drive and . . . .

Mr. D____: Now, that's the craziest idea we've heard yet.

Chairman: Let's get down to cases here, ladies and gentlemen. This meeting was called to talk over a proposal of great importance and to see if we could clear the air a bit, and decide where our groups will stand when the proposal comes to a vote next week. We have heard several questions raised and answered. I have a feeling that we are a little closer together. Now let's get on a bit farther. Any other discussion?

MR. C____: There's one more thing I'd like to have cleared up a bit. I know now that the site of the pool will save us money because it can be obtained almost as a gift, but have you folks had your figures worked out by experts? Are you sure the sum, if it should be voted, will cover the costs?

MR. B____: We appreciate that question. Yes, we think we have adequate assurance on the figures. Two firms that specialize in such projects have worked out estimates independently and they both feel that we'll get what we need for $150,000.

MR. L____: I agree. It's a fine plan.

MR. N____: Would you review for us just what the pool will add up to — size, water supply, etc.?

MR. B____: Yes, the pool will be constructed of concrete 180 by 60 feet — with a graduated depth to accommodate swimmers and divers of varying skills. It will have concrete aprons and the latest in dressing houses, with showers and disinfectant foot baths. The water will undergo constant controlled chlorination. Our town will have a swimming plant of which it can be proud — and there are no gimmicks — no extras. We have checked on all these matters again and again.

Good job of calling to order and summarizing the progress

Note B____ is no longer being a mother hen about his proposal

L____ is a yes man. Notice his earlier comment.

A neat bit of expediting. This question invites an answer.

11 TO TAKE PART

IN A JOB INTERVIEW

OCCASION: Any situation in which it is necessary to put your best foot forward — primarily the job interview. Usually this situation involves an audience of one and rarely more than four or five.

DESIRED RESPONSE: To impress the listener favorably with your personality, training, and competence.

METHODS: The key to face-to-face interviews is that they are face-to-face. The interviewer very likely has all the essential facts about you. He has had them for days. You are here across the desk from him because he feels there are certain things about you that he can check better if he can see you and hear you. Remember, then, the important things are how you look and how you sound. With that firmly in mind you are bound to get more satisfaction out of interviews.

Relax. Don't freeze. This does not mean hooking a leg over the chair or sprawling forward on your prospective employer's desk, although either of these is better than to sit dry-lipped and fluttery. As a matter of fact, a middle course is desirable. Work for a combination of confidence and restraint. Remember the object is not to sweep your listener off his feet with a detailed and dramatic recital of your qualifications but to provide information when it is called for. Job interviewers have been struck, but not always favorably struck, by the increasing tendency of young prospects to pounce aggressively upon them and interview them. Many a prospect charges into the interviewer's office — balances on the boss's desk with one foot swinging and cross-examines him on the job. "What can I expect from this outfit? How long do I have to wait to get it? How much free play will be given my talents with you people?" And so on and on. This doesn't work very well with this generation of employers. Maybe later. Admittedly this approach is not altogether without its good side, but the wise interviewee will use it sparingly.

Look the part. Neatness and good taste in dress, the well-groomed look, have more impact upon the listener than he himself would probably admit. They suggest certain strongly favorable qualities of mind.

If you are the prospective employer, don't use unkind "torture chamber" devices such as the armless chair facing the light, etc. After all, ability to remain game in the face of rudeness is only one of the qualities you are looking for.

The following comments on job interviewing are worth your special attention. They were written by Dr. Lewis R. Toll, Chairman of the Department of Business Education at Illinois State Normal University, and President of the National Association for Business Teacher Education.

"Since first impressions are very important the applicant should be appropriately groomed for the interview. He should be impeccably clean and carefully dressed, but not overdressed. His manner should be relaxed and friendly, yet attentive and respectful.

"Upon meeting the employing official for the first time, the applicant should give his name slowly and distinctly and immediately state that he is interested in the job that is open or might be open. The applicant should be natural and not give the impression that he is trying to sell himself. His attitude should be that the interview is for the purpose of determining whether the position's opportunities and responsibilities are in line with his interests and abilities. He should look at the eyes of the employer most of the time he is talking with him if he can do so without giving the appearance of staring.

"The applicant should neither be reticent nor aggressive. He should answer questions with more than a 'Yes' or a 'No,' but he should keep in mind that the employer likes to conduct the interview. After the employer has given some information about the position that is open, the applicant may ask questions about the job and about the company. Most worthwhile positions today are of a permanent nature and employers are seeking workers who plan to stay with the firm for years. They look with favor upon prospective employees who manifest a genuine interest in such things as the kind of business the company is engaged in, the personnel policies of the company, and the promotional possibilities of the job.

"Many young job applicants tend to speak disparagingly of their work experience. This is a mistake regardless of how menial the applicant's jobs have been so long as they were legal and made a contribution to society. It is a sign of lack of appreciation for good experience to make such statements as 'I have just clerked in my father's store' or 'The only selling I have done is house-to-house canvassing.'

"It is also a mistake to speak with dissatisfaction about any employers the applicant has had. An employer prefers persons who have enjoyed the other jobs they have had.

"The job applicant does not tell the employer what he cannot do well. He may tell about his proficiencies and his interests, and his preferences. If he is asked about his ability in an area wherein he does not excel, he should say that he has more ability and interest in other areas.

"The employer is pleased to find a person who is self-confident without being 'cocky,' who is enthusiastic without being 'showy,' who is ambitious without being aggressive."

Some Don'ts

Don't make it a monologue.

Don't forget to stop whatever you are saying in order to answer questions.

Don't overdo the go-getter, nose-to-nose approach at interviews — after all, hypnosis is not the object.

Don't neglect pre-interview analysis of your prospective employer or buyer.

Don't forget, the interviewer brought you here not only to ask you questions but to *see* you and *hear* you. Look your best and sound your best.

The following sample job interview might be helpful.

A kind employer will indicate a specific chair

EMPLOYER: Hello! You're Mr. X_____. I'm glad you're here. Sit down. Did you get in this morning?

MR. X——: Thank you. Yes, I came in on the 10 o'clock train.

EMPLOYER: A good fast train; I often use it myself. I still shy away from flying whenever I can avoid it. Old-fashioned I guess. Ever been in our town before?

MR. X——: Yes, I've been here several times but never looked around much. This is my first visit in your building, however.

EMPLOYER: Yes, yes. Well, how do you like our home office? We're very proud of it. And that brings us to your reason for being here. I understand that you'd like to join our company? Is that right? Now let me see, just what sort of job were you interested in?

Much of this chitchat is inconclusive. Its purpose is to give the prospect a chance to get his breath. It may go on a long time depending upon where a lead-in occurs.

MR. X——: I hope eventually to go into the special field of group insurance. I understand from my correspondence with your Mr. J—— that you are at present carrying on a training program for young men in that kind of work and I thought this was the place to come. Ever since I was in high school I have thought of insurance as my chosen vocation, and . . . .

EMPLOYER: Fine! Have you had any experience in the life insurance field, Mr. X——?

This seems a trifle over-done. It also fails to convey any useful information. The prospect was probably too nervous and too eager.

MR. X——: Frankly no I have not, but I have had several courses in selling at the University and I have prepared myself . . . .

EMPLOYER: Have you had any kind of experience in selling in any line?

MR. X——: Well, not exactly. Oh, I did work for eight months as a counter salesman in a men's clothing store, but . . . .

EMPLOYER: That's pretty good. How did you like it? Do you feel you were pretty successful at that work? After all . . . .

Don't minimize your previous experience. Report it and let the interviewer judge its value and pertinence.

MR. X——: Oh, I did pretty well, I guess. It wasn't very much like insurance, of course.

A nice gesture here. It often pays to encourage the applicant.

EMPLOYER: Did you like meeting the people? It seems to me you are a person who wouldn't have any trouble with that. But group insurance is not just the same thing, naturally. Ordinarily in our group program you will be working as one of a team once you get into it. The problems of meeting people remain pretty much the same, however. Do you understand just what group insurance is, and what's involved in this work?

MR. X_____:I am sure I have a lot to learn here at the home office, but I have studied up on this particular branch of insurance. I understand that your company requires a six months training course here at the home office. Now if . . . .

EMPLOYER: There is such a course, yes. While the pay during the period isn't high, our trainees have been able to get along quite well. Are you married, Mr. X_____?

Don't be carried away on this one

MR. X_____: Yes, I'm married. Was married four years ago and have two fine children, Chucky and Tiny. They're . . . .

An effort to give applicant a breather. If the prospect doesn't know an end run from a punt it won't help much, of course, but it's still a good risk with most men.

EMPLOYER: That's fine. Now, we have your records for high school and college have we not? And your credentials. You will, of course, be able to take the company's personnel tests this afternoon, Mr. X_____? By the way, you went to M_____ State didn't you? I went to M_____ U. We used to beat you in football in those days. Don't seem to be doing it very often lately. I'd like to get away for more games. Are you much of a fan on football?

He fumbled it! Is the boss a loafer?

MR. X_____: Personally I don't get much fun out of football. Never got to the games. I was too busy most of the time trying to get through college. I do like golf, but . . . .

194

EMPLOYER: Well, we all have our pet likes and dislikes. Now I want you to go down to Mr. J——— in personnel. Thank you very much for coming in. I've enjoyed our talk. Good bye.

12 TO BE A TOASTMASTER

OCCASION: The after-dinner situation with speakers.

DESIRED RESPONSE: Pleasant atmosphere; a fast moving program.

METHODS: There are several ways of looking at the job of toastmaster, depending pretty much upon one's experience with members of the species. They may be classified as follows:

The "surgical expert" type who snips skillfully here and there almost without pain, and then presents the victim to the audience.

The "play-back" type who repeats, without any particular improvement, most of what the preceding speaker has said.

The "dog-with-a-bone" type who feels some responsibility for insulting each speaker, bruising his feelings, and sometimes, I am afraid, scaring him half to death.

Lastly, the "hundred-proof" type. This type — by no means rare — gets himself into such a condition before taking over that everything seems funny to him. Such a speaker cannot miss — if he can't roll them in the aisles, he can at least put them under the table.

Actually, the duties of a good toastmaster are few and well defined: He must set the tone of the gathering; he must keep things moving; and he must provide transitions. He will, of course, want a supply of stories. It is not perfectly clear why the joke has come to loom so large in after-dinner situations, but it has, and the after-dinner guest has learned to face it.

A final reminder to toastmasters is probably worthwhile. Stories resemble people in two significant ways: First, their ultimate success depends a great deal upon how they were brought up, and second, no matter how we hate to admit it, both show signs of decreased effectiveness as they get older.

Some Don'ts

Don't forget that some of the speakers you introduce need help,
  not abuse.
Don't feel obliged to limit your stories to the obscene.
Don't forget to keep things moving.

13 TO MAKE AN

AFTER–DINNER SPEECH

occasion: Before dinner audiences. It is wise to assume that most of your listeners have eaten at least to capacity and are in a somewhat torpid state.

desired response: To add to the feeling of well-being. A secondary aim could be to inform or persuade. It is quite evident that a serious, not to say grim, purpose frequently motivates speakers when they talk before after-dinner audiences. You have been a fortunate listener, indeed, if you have not suffered through more than one ponderous expository or informative speech at the dinner table. Nevertheless, though speakers will doubtless go on delving into the Russian-American problem, disposal of the atom bomb, and analysis of the business cycle, the dinner table is not the place for such heavy dissertations.

methods: To hark back to what we have said about the desired response, it is well first to remember to keep the treatment light in this situation. The speaker is up against what may best be called a physiological limitation. With the system of the listener busy, or at least preoccupied with the business of digestion, it is wise not to expect too much mental alertness. The audience is not so likely to resent serious topics as simply not to make much of them. The after-dinner speaker should not abandon all arrangement and intelligent outline in his effort to avoid solemnity. We have all listened with something approaching disgust to the men whose after-dinner speech consists simply of standing up and being "reminded." Despite the fact that some men have built reputations as wits and after-dinner speakers on this technique, it is still pretty shaky. The speaker simply looks at the audience, beams and is suddenly reminded in a disconcerting and frequently unflattering way of a funny story. This story reminds him of another one. From there on the technique is self-perpetuating. The things that some jokes will remind speakers of frequently defy belief. Rather than making your after-dinner contributions simply an amusing story or an ill-assorted string of them, you should work for an outline from which to suspend a few jokes or witticisms, and this outline should have some connection with the occasion. See Part Two, "Some Good Attention-Getters," for added comment on stories.

The humorous element in an after-dinner speech may come from the witticism or wisecrack as well as from the story. If the speaker has the knack of making his remarks witty, this method is actually to be preferred to the story. Unfortunately, most of us don't have the knack. And an oft-told tale can scarcely fall flatter than a wisecrack which fails to come off.

It may be necessary to intersperse a few serious comments in your after-dinner speech but it is generally wiser, and always kinder, to avoid them.

Some Don'ts

Don't be "reminded" too often.
Don't strain for a laugh.
Don't use off-color stories in mixed groups.
Don't talk too long.
Don't laugh louder than your listeners.
Don't feel compelled to make yourself or someone else at your table the hero of each story.

14 TO TALK

ON THE TELEPHONE

DESIRED RESPONSE: Understanding of exactly what you said and some feeling of direct personal communication.

METHODS: The telephone, considering the vast extent of its use, proves an irritating and highly unsatisfactory instrument to a lot of people. Most of that thwarted feeling that telephone conversation so frequently gives is the fault of the speaker. A great deal of fun is frequently made of people who shout into the telephone, but certainly people who mutter or mumble or whisper into the phone are the greater evil. In other words, loudness is absolutely essential if you are going to be sure to be heard. This does not mean bellowing at the top of your lungs, but it does mean a little more sustained volume than would be necessary across a table.

Most important, of course, is careful articulation. This is recognized directly in the recommendations made for pronouncing "nine" as "ni-un," and "five" as "fi-ev." Careful stress of consonants is essential on the telephone as perhaps nowhere else, but, with careful enunciation, the man talking on the phone should be sure not to slur over or partially drop certain words — a habit many of us have in face-to-face conversation. Some investigation seems to indicate that the average listener does not consciously react to more than about two words out of three; but the man on the phone can never be sure which of his words the listener will choose to react to.

We have been speaking thus far, of course, of telephone talk as an act of communication in which the ideas must be put across in an unmistakable fashion. At the same time, one of the special virtues of using the phone in many situations lies in the fact that it gives the listener a chance to hear the "sound of your voice." It provides an element of the personal. There is no doubt at all that if one is to be careful about articulation it will be a little harder for the personal flavor to come through, but it may still do so. Some speakers can, in other words, be "visited with" on the phone as easily as not. There is no reason why anyone should squeeze all the personality out of his voice and become a lifeless, staccato machine.

On the question of what to talk about on the phone it is hard to be specific, but the following advice is useful. First, name yourself. Second, check on your listener. Third, say what you called to say. Fourth, get it said quickly and in concise language.

Some Don'ts

Don't forget that you're talking into a telephone.

Don't overlook the possibility of mechanical difficulties at either or both ends of the line.

Don't get too close to the speaker (nor too far away for that matter).

Don't forget, if you are indulging in "asides," to keep them distinct from the remarks intended for the listener.

WITHOUT OFFENSE

OCCASION: Before anyone who needs adverse criticism, but whose good will is worth keeping.

DESIRED RESPONSE: Enthusiastic, or at least friendly, acceptance of correction or improvement.

METHODS: Many men in the administrative end of industry and the professions have asked about this problem. Dozens of them have unhesitatingly picked it as their toughest speaking assignment. The following suggestions should be helpful.

First, be sure your suggestions for change are called for. The job is going to be delicate enough when your criticisms are founded solidly in fact and experience. It's doubtful if unfair or unjustified criticism can ever be made palatable.

Second, remember audience analysis. How you go about criticism will depend a great deal upon the person whose work is to be questioned. Some folks can take it better than others; some are thick-skinned and others thin-skinned. What's more, the temperamental man may be a very useful man. A knowledge of his staff will, of course, make the assignment much easier for the average administrator as time goes on.

But to get on with specific suggestions. I think the best one can be labeled the "Don't make the same mistake I made" approach. Let the man know that you tried the offending technique yourself earlier in your career and found that it didn't work. This puts you in the same boat as the other fellow — it actually eliminates disapproval from your comments.

Another I like to call the "I'm not disgusted" approach. In this one you tease the recipient a bit, tell a joke, let him know you're not mad at anybody. This is useful with the man who lives in terror of the boss's wrath, and a surprising number of people do. Such a man may be disintegrated by too blunt criticism. He may clam up and never contribute again, and this could be unfortunate.

Another worth-while technique we can label the "Look at it my way" approach. Here you invite the man who has made the offending proposal or taken the wrong course of action to talk over the matter from your standpoint — to put himself in your place. By this means the change becomes a cooperative action and there can be no sting in it.

There are occasions wherein the best approach involves helping the man to discover the desirable changes for himself. Early in my teaching career I had occasion to work for an administrator who stood guard over his prerogatives like a brooding hen. He seemed impervious to suggestion until we finally discovered a surprisingly effective approach. Whenever we came up with a good idea we would present it somewhat as follows: "Some of us have been wondering, Mr. _____, why it wouldn't be good to develop the idea you brought up at the winter meeting concerning the creation of a new department?" Thereafter our man would take off with the idea, and since it was now his own, he would see that it was carried out fully and just as we had wanted it.

A final suggestion is one that might seem a bit obvious to some of my readers but is nevertheless a device of long standing. It extends the ancient truism that more flies can be caught with sugar than with vinegar to argue that flies caught by the sugar will stay for the vinegar. Compliment the man on what he has done well before you call attention to what he is doing badly. Some people have actually reduced this to a formula which calls for two compliments for two adverse criticisms, etc.

It might be well in closing this section to submit that only a society of ill-adjusted personalities makes all this deviousness necessary. We all long for a day when forthright and helpful criticism can be directed at the work of relaxed and well-adjusted people without fear of consequences.

Some Dont's

Don't criticize without long consideration.
Don't avoid your duty to criticize from fear of hurting feelings.
Don't confine your criticism to negative remarks.
Don't attempt criticism till you know your man.

Index

INDEX